;0;9;4

THE FEMALE HERO
IN WOMEN'S LITERATURE AND POETRY

Susan A. Lichtman

Women's Studies
Volume 10

The Edwin Mellen Press
Lewiston/Queenston/Lampeter

Library of Congress Cataloging-in-Publication Data

Lichtman, Susan A.
  The female hero in women's literature and poetry / Susan A.
Lichtman.
      p.   cm. -- (Women's studies ; v. 10)
  Includes bibliographical references (p.   ).
  ISBN 0-7734-8796-4 (hard)
    1. English literature--Women authors--History and criticism.
2. American literature--Women authors--History and criticism.
3. Feminism and literature--Great Britain--History. 4. Feminism and
literature--United States--History. 5. Women and literature--United
States--History. 6. Women and literature--Great Britain--History.
7. Heroines in literature. 8. Sex role in literature. I. Title.
II. Series: Women's studies (Lewiston, N.Y.) ; v. 10.
PR111.L5 1996
820.9'352042--dc20   95-43269
                                                          CIP

This is volume 10 in the continuing series
Women's Studies
Volume 10 ISBN 0-7734-8796-4
WS Series ISBN 0-88946-118-X

A CIP catalog record for this book is available from the British Library.

The Edwin Mellen Press   The Edwin Mellen Press
        Box 450   Box 67
  Lewiston, New York   Queenston, Ontario
   USA 14092-0450   CANADA L0S 1L0

The Edwin Mellen Press, Ltd.
Lampeter, Dyfed, Wales
UNITED KINGDOM SA48 7DY

Printed in the United States of America

To my teachers and my students

Contents

Foreword

I hope that my work will enrich the dialogues between scholars, students, and searchers on their own journeys toward self actualization. This book, used in conjunction with *Life Stages of Woman's Heroic Journey: A Study of the Origins of the Great Goddess Archetype*, can open areas of study and discussion about the woman hero and her quest in women's literature and poetry. Because literature forever frames our views of ourselves, the archetypal approach to its interpretation can demonstrate the importance to society of the hero and the lessons learned on the personal quest.

Because women need to see themselves as heroes and their experiences as valid, the importance of the study of women's literature and poetry is necessary for all students in order to better communicate the differing experiences of life for women and men. The validation of the woman hero will allow for better dialogues between the sexes, as we strive for a better understanding of all people and of all human experiences.

I have always endorsed an interdisciplinary study of literature, using history, psychology, mythology, anthropology, astronomy, archaeology, and sociology as bases for understanding the myriad of literary expressions about the human condition in all its rich varieties. My work specifically centers on the woman hero in women's literature and poetry, and the monomyth of self actualization that runs deeply throughout all these writings. I also hope that by re-visioning women's myths, we restore, or re-member, a sense of heroism for our own mothers, daughters, and grandmothers. The essays included in this book are intended as a starting point for the further investigation of mythological archetypes and templates in women's literature and poetry.

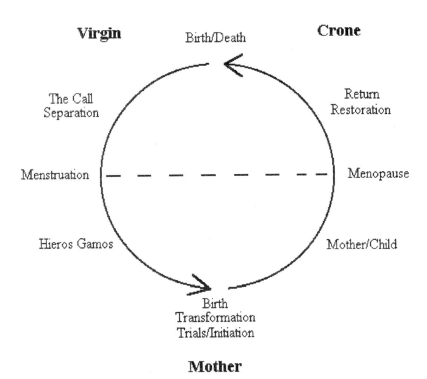

The Female Hero's
Journey of
Self Actualization

Prologue: Woman as Hero in Twentieth Century Literature

There are several characteristics defined by feminist scholars as particular to the genre of women's writing. From the rituals of daily life to the appearance of shadows or feelings of otherness, women writers display the delicate intricacies of women's lives. When these characteristics are mated with archetypal symbolism and sign systems, the results are rich and varied stories about women characters who embody our own personal hopes, fears, and frustrations and development. Instead of the traditional endings of marriage or death for their women characters, women writers tend to leave their heroes with conditional endings that serve to leave the possibilities open for both character and reader. But all women writers concern themselves with the search for the authentic self or self actualization. If we include feminist archetypal theory, then we can see these characters develop and grow through the three stages of woman's physical and psychological growth: virgin, mother, crone. It is through this growth that women advance through their own hero cycle, a cycle that begins in the virgin stage, descends into the mother stage, and then reemerges as wise crone by the end of the cycle. But unlike the male paradigm for the hero tales, the crone not only reasserts the history and the lessons of her life, but she also connects back to the virgin stage as mentor or teacher for other young women beginning their own hero cycle. As a result, there is a continuum of woman's experience that is shared and valued even within (or maybe in spite of) patriarchal society.

Women writers tend to break stereotypes and historical presumptions by presenting strong women characters who, following the recipe of the bildungsroman, move from ignorance to knowledge, from inexperience to experience. Their heroes almost always appear in social contexts, reaffirming the concept of the intricate web of relationships through which women perceive reality. The communities of women, the sisterhoods shared among women, become of paramount importance when viewed as part of a developmental process. If women could define that process as a sort of mega-myth for all women, then we can see the process happening in novels of development written by women for women. Joseph Campbell has already defined the mega-myth for male heroes in *The Hero With a Thousand Faces*. He did so by identifying male heroes in mythologies from all over the world; he then identified all the commonalties shared by these male heroes as they move through their lives. I have attempted to do the same with my book, *Life Stages of Woman's Heroic Journey*, in which ancient mythologies that concern themselves with women heroes (Demeter, Inanna) are examined for the shared characteristics among many different goddesses. The difference between the female and male heroes can be explained as the difference between mortal life and the eternal soul. In ancient human societies before the discovery of paternity and development of private property, women were perceived as immortal creatures because they could give birth to themselves through their daughters; men, on the other hand, were perceived as strictly mortal beings. These perceptions were severely altered once paternity was established, and men could now identify their own children as long as the mothers were isolated from all other men.

Because the status of women in patriarchal societies is so very low, they are only perceived by the dominant males as peripheral to human existence. The true human experience had to be the male's experience. And so women were pushed to the margins of human history with no story of their own. At least as far as most men thought. But women have always told stories, even if they only told them to other women, and even if those stories were not believed to be deep, accurate, or educational. Oh, that's just another old wives' tale. Yet, those stories came to strengthen the bonds between women because of the shared nature of their experiences. And experiences give rise to stories, which in turn validates that experience as worthwhile and as particularly human. For women to write their own stories, sing their own songs, dance their own dances, fulfills the concept of being women. Without articulation, the self perishes. Experience then loses any value. It is in this sense then that it becomes of paramount importance to hear the stories, to read the experiences, to sing the songs, so women can dance their own dances. And what better place then the novels of development, the articulation of the woman hero's life span, to inspire us to further study, and valorize, the experiences of over half the world's population.

Novels of development have long been seen as attempts by artists and writers to demonstrate the growth and integration of the hero on a individual quest for self discovery. The knowledge and wisdom gained along the way is then used by the hero to re-educate and redirect society into the newly discovered methods of group dynamics and personal responsibility. The polarity of society versus the individual is renegotiated in every generation. Writers and poets have understood the delicate balance that must be maintained between the two in order to preserve the idea of the social with the idea of individual development and accomplishment.

When novels of development are combined with feminist archetypal theory, the results for women are manifested in a pattern of life stages that mark a woman's growth and maturation from the uninitiated and self absorbed youth to the trials of reintegration into the social fabric and finally into a persona of wisdom and direction as legacy. In ancient matri-focused cultures, this can be seen in the goddess myths in which women were perceived as the original heroes -- the movers and shakers -- of their societies. This story line, along with so much more, was stolen and reintegrated with the appropriate gender change from female to male once the patriarchal philosophy took hold. As a result, when we think of heroes today, we usually envision males at the forefront of the hero myth with the females taking their place as the originators of the hero through their maternity, or as the obstacles the hero must overcome and/or destroy represented by female sexuality, or finally as the end goal, the prize, the *hieros gamos* the hero wins by asserting himself successfully through the hero cycle.

It has only been relatively recently that women have had an opportunity to insist on seeing themselves as the heroes of their own lives in their own societies. In traditional novels of development written by men about women, there are only two ways for a woman hero to end her story: marriage or death. But women writers have long sensed other endings. They write of female characters who assert themselves well beyond the traditional endings, well beyond the limits of imposed patriarchal order. To understand these female heroes and their accomplishments, archetypal theory provides the basic alphabet by which we may decipher the codes and signs within the text. We begin to see that these female heroes were there all along written into the subversive margins of traditional stories, or more recently, the modern mosaic of twentieth century literature.

To begin, we must have an understanding of the theoretical basis to a feminist archetypal reading. In *Life Stages of Women's Heroic* Journey, I have outlined the foundation for a new reading of traditional signs and symbols based on ancient goddess characters and their myths. This foundation can be expanded as various novels of development, as well as other writings by women, are analyzed to discover and integrate into modern life the hero myth for women.

There are three basic stages for women's heroic journey through life. They are, in terms the ancients have long associated with the Goddess: virgin, mother, crone. These three stages taken together represent the whole span of a woman's life from ignorance and passion to the birth of the social being and finally, the arrival at wisdom and legacy for the future generations. All three stages carry their own signs, symbols, and even colors, to identify the successful passage through each stage.

The first phase of development for women is the virgin phase, virgin meaning woman unto herself. The female hero begins her life's adventures with the separation from her mother and the onset of menstruation. There is usually the presence of an older woman who acts as a guide and a tutor for the young initiate into womanhood. The descent of the female hero then is a descent into self, an acknowledgment of the magical and mystical processes of the female body. The purpose of the descent into self is for the female to become self aware and self involved with the promise of her body. While in that descent, our young hero may experience a *hieros gamos*, a sacred marriage, which becomes a part of her education, but by no means the extent of it. The symbols associated with this phase can be applied to the season of spring, enclosures, and images of becoming: budding vegetation, blooming flowers and trees, secrets hidden in containers like boxes, pockets, jewel cases, secret rooms, hidden treasures, and finally the color of white.

The second phase belongs to the mother stage of development. Even though this phase is described in terms of maternity, that which is nurtured or created may or may not include children. Other creations, such as art, music, poetry, social criticisms, inventions, corporations, businesses, are just as valid. The focus of the mother phase is to bring the hero out of self absorbtion and self development and into a more social realm of community; the creations of the mothers allow or ensure the perpetuation of the human species. The concept of community may be as varied as a particular family or town, village, society, sisterhood, or any group of people who by their coming together strengthen the chances of human survival. The mother's color is red for blood, sexuality, life-force, birth, or rebirth. Her season is the summer and the nurturance of its growth. Symbols can be containers of all types, houses, the process of naming, harvests, water, oceans, signs of change or transformations, sacrifice of the personal for the communal, relative boundaries, and parenting. In this phase of self in relation to society, the mother learns and accepts a certain degree of selflessness which allows her society continuation.

The last phase is that of the crone, harbinger of death and the new life or generation that always follows. This self in relation to eternity phase begins with the menopause, a cessation of blood flow that the ancients interpreted as the beginning of wisdom. The crone keeps the history of her family or community. She also must pass on to the next generation the stories and lessons of her group's past. She becomes the sage-femme to the virgin about to embark on her life's journey. Her seasons are autumn and/or winter, and her color is black. Symbols may include white horses, birds, images of flying, witches, fairy godmothers, crossroads, dogs, thresholds, and the blending or blurring of boundaries. She becomes the mistress of two worlds: life and death. She is herself legacy.

The novel of development, or the bildungsroman, has a deeply mythical background as well. It is inexorably linked with the hero's cycle of movement from ignorance to knowledge, from inexperience to experience. The ancients used the hero cycle to justify or rationalize human existence and mortality. For males, this mythical storyline is bound with the adolescent belief in personal immortality which is tested and retested, and finally honed into the adult acceptance of mortality and human limitations. But for females, the hero cycle is connected to endurance, and ultimately, the survival of the human condition. The original hero cycle was female in origin. Linked to the common ancient belief of earthly existence as female (Mother Nature, Gaia), the female hero cycle exemplified the growth and maturation of the human being through experience. This growth is marked by the female stages of virgin, mother, crone through which the female hero changed and developed into a complex, multifaceted selfhood which celebrated humanity and its generations. Death was not seen as a personal ending, but as a new beginning for the next generation. It was as necessary as winter, as necessary as the old making way for the young, but with the legacy of wisdom and history that only the aged could provide. To ignore that history or that legacy was, and is, to deny the experience and knowledge of past generations. Forget the past, as Santayanna would agree, and we condemn the future to unnecessary and degenerative repetition. Poets understand this as well as writers. As the prophets of each generation, they seek to remind us of our pasts and the vast stores of wisdom to be found there.

For women to be reminded of their past is to place in their hands the stores of wisdom which reminds them of the rich legacies that have gone before. That wisdom reconnects them and their legacies of experience, of emotion, and of personal empowerment. With male texts, that wisdom is written in the margins of the not said, the not explained or voiced. But in women's texts, that same wisdom appears in bold faced type.

For women to see themselves as heroes of their own life experiences is itself a liberating prospect. It allows us a valuation of personal experience, a valuation of those details of life so traditionally seen as women's venue. But it also allows women to view themselves as complex, ever-changing human beings. In child development, no one stage of growth is rated more important than any other stage of growth. Instead, each stage is necessary to the development of the child into an adult. To miss a stage or to ignore a stage in that development creates a young adult who is less than whole. Male children and female children experience their developmental stages differently; for example, they learn and express language at different rates. This doesn't make one sex better than the other; it just means that the development of males and females from children to adults occurs at different rates and speeds. These differing rates continue for humans through adolescence. Adolescence for both sexes carries some of the same experiences, but these experiences and growth rates differ between females and males. So why should the one compelling storyline about male heroes be interpreted the same way for males and for females?

The hero cycle is both the integration of the self into a whole individual who then must find expression as part of the collective society. The stories tell us that it is a fine line of balance that must be maintained between the social and the individual. It is that balance that provides the tension for the story. The hero myths are retold in various versions for each generation because that fine line of balance shifts for every generation. There are universals that survive the test of time, but for the most part, each sex must renegotiate the boundaries and the limitations of the personal within the social. In our post-modernist world of fragmentations, these boundaries and limitations are most problematic. There are very few institutions left that command the authority of the past. These institutions vary considerably depending on the cultural areas under investigation. But the universals have survived. It is the recognition of these universals that brings the hero myths back to life, back to the legitimacy of interpreting the human condition.

These universals are locked within the archetypal language of images, signs, and symbols that have survived time's passage. They enjoy a kind of primal recognition despite their cultural interpretations. For Jung, they are a part of the collective unconscious, a universal memory of our earliest experiences shared by all humans. Birth, love, death, time, and eternity are among the subjects of the archetypes. But so are the sex coded memories of individual progress and change. Because these archetypes survive each generation, an examination of them releases the hero cycle inherent in their interpretation. And as the male hero cycle can deal with the male's lessons of the distant and ancient past, so too can the female hero myths release the same power of identification for women. Not as mothers, sisters, wives, betrotheds, or grandmothers of, but as individuals seeking the same personal integration of self despite the social relationships and connectors.

The purpose here is to propose a new, working model for change and development that can contribute a sense of interconnectedness to the social world as well as contributing to the potential of women as they see themselves as heroes of their own life stories.

Women writers and poets recognize the difference between women being defined as biology and being defined by social construct. They push against the boundaries of perceived realities and gender norms. They weave a complex tapestry of anecdotes, images, and stories that represent the whole of woman's life. They see humanity as more than androcentric; they see humans as more than social or cultural constructs. Some basic characteristics of women's writings may include shadows or feelings of otherness, communities of women as valuable sub-cultures, conditional endings of novels, rituals of daily life, domestic issues mirroring political issues and thus reforming the public through private experience. Since all women share a certain degree of ritualized physical/personal rites like menstruation, pregnancy, birth, lactation, and menopause, women writers recognize these experiences as habits of living that are traditionally hidden from males or the dominent social structure. But for women, these experiences are often shared among themselves. As a result, this mostly oral tradition for women becomes a vast storehouse of lessons learned to be passed down from generation to generation as almost survivalist information thus continuing the circularity of female heritage. Many times, the structure of a novel or a poem will mimic this circularity by connecting the end of the work to its own beginning. Finally, the most prevalent characteristic of women writers' work is their search for the authentic female self.

The search for self is the refusal to be victimized or stereotyped even by one's own shadow or sense of otherness. The hero quests after pyschic wholeness and purpose. Even language and its functions becomes a complex symbol system of elemental archetypes and myths that are manipulated by the writer's pen to provide meaning to the the female experience. Images used on this search can include mirrors or bodies of water that can reflect the hero's perceptions of self. Other topics covered by women writers include the examination of oppression by sex or by sex and race, women's work and issues of domestic politics, sisterhoods and communities of women, marriage, social responsibility versus individual freedoms, gender identity in relation to law and politics, and questioning the validity of patriarchal histories which results in shifts of gender emphasis to include women's experiences with biological, cultural, psychological, and linguistical definitions and constraints.

The themes used by women writers reflect various states of transformation or metamorphosis. There is a sense of crossing boundaries or discovering secret passages. One of woman's oldest traditions with the concept of transformation can be found in the ancient Greek Thesmophorus festival. This celebration consisted of three parts: the Kathodos and Anados (the down-going and the up-coming), Nestia (fasting) and Kallegeneia (the fair birth). The festival's name means Demeter-Who-Established-the-Custom, and the participants of the festival mimicked the myth of Demeter and Persephone. Each phase of the festival also corresponds to the virgin, mother, crone aspects of woman's life. Because men were forbidden to be anywhere close to the festival's participants, many of the ritual's secrets were never recorded.

The recognition of the power of language is another strong element in women's writing. Even the power to name, to define concepts and patterns, becomes a central issue in defining ourselves. Names and the process of naming is a form of owning or personalizing an experience or the self. Most of what women learn and pass on to others is oral/aural, spoken or heard. It is important to understand the orality of women's legacy because it is partially comprised of the necessities for survival. Humans have to impart to their young the rules and regulations about safety and survival, what can be eaten and what must be avoided, what cures and what kills. We may refer to it with its politically correct nomenclature -- networking -- but this supposedly modern concept is really an ancient practice for women in any culture. And teaching the next generation to survive   has   always   been   women's   concern.

Tears of Rhiannon:
The Origins of Patriarchal Power in *The Mabinogion*

Fear of the archaic mother turns out to be essentially fear of her generative power.

- Julia Kristeva

Every patriarchal society has its own literature of origins that chronicles the cultural and religious beginnings of great and glorious heroes. These heroes overcome enormous obstacles in establishing their power and authority over a people. With the scholarship done in the last hundred years or so, we now know this authority was wrested from the hands of other cultures already in existence for thousands of years. These highly developed cultures were based on matri-lineal groups of people whose deities comprised the major aspects of the Great Goddess. Within these groups, women were considered mystical beings with tremendous authority over the seasons of the year, the fertility of the land, and the survival of their children. The goddesses themselves were considered eternal beings with the capacity of reproducing themselves; every daughter was her mother, every mother was her crone, every crone was her daughter, and so the female cycle would renew itself with the passing of every generation. The advent of two remarkable events of male consciousness inevitably led to the overthrow of the matri-lineal groups: the awareness of paternity and the origins of personal property. Both events gave males the authority they needed to attain control, usually violent, and to establish their own lines of succession and inheritance in terms of property and kinship. It is on these lines that modern society claims its descendance.

But what of the matri-lineal groups so ruthlessly displaced? What of the goddesses and their priestesses and their philosophies about the human condition? What of the women and their place in this new order? Modern scholarship has found their remnants in almost every area searched: archeology, anthropology, socio-anthropology, psychology, and ancient, as well as modern, literature all retain the vestiges of a female origin of life, culture, and society. The story of their overthrow, their isolation from the centers of the new male power, and their devaluation in society from goddesses holding the power of life and death within their bodies to mere vessels for male seed with no existing consciousness of their own hides within every literature of cultural origin from all over the world. It is only recently that feminist scholars have learned to tune their ears and their eyes toward the goddesses' faint cries of anguish and sorrow that echo in every text codifying patriarchal power. Even though these texts were written by males, usually attached to the religious centers of the patriarchal gods, the symbolism and the language retained from the older oral tradition give indications of the displaced female shadows that have haunted the texts, seeking reparations for the ancient indignities suffered by them and by their daughters. It is in this spirit, then, that I demonstrate the female presence displaced and denigrated in *The Mabinogion* as a text of patriarchal origins for the early Welsh people.

The process of revising female consciousness, as imagined by the emergent clerical aesthetic of literacy and the authority of the written word, begins with the removal of the goddess as a self-rejuvenating life-force and her transformation into mere vegetable matter created and imbued with life by male agents of the patriarchal divine. This process is recorded and encoded in the text of *The Mabinogion* in very much the same way it is encoded and recorded in other patristic canonical literature used to authorize and legitimize the assumption of control by the emerging patriarchal culture over the more simple, matri-focal society. The usurpation of the birth process from female to male control, the reordering of rank and power within the governing body of that society, and the reconstituted and redefined symbols of the female result in the arrest of female development and the devaluation of the female principle within society from divine entity to personal property.

In interpreting the symbolism used in ancient literature and passed on for hundreds of years through the oral tradition, it becomes necessary to rely on psychological theories regarding the conscious and unconscious and the means by which the human mind records its own experiences and fears through symbolism. The two poles of psychology to which most scholars are drawn are the Freudian interpretation and the Jungian interpretation of symbolism. At this point in time, most feminist scholars are working diligently to establish a particular female psychology that would take into account the experience of the female as unique and individual from the male. In this regard then, the interpretations of symbols may vary even within feminist scholarship, but the entree into an analysis of a complete female consciousness has at least begun. Both schools are represented here in order to open the text to further research and interpretation.

The Mabinogion links together the preexistant mythology of the earliest goddess worshipping people, the initial incursions of the patriarchal culture and its subsequent overthrow of the earlier matri-focal society, and the pale overlay of the Christian cleric and his new written word. In writing this adventure of human development, the cleric retained the oral flavor of the stories with their mnenomic rhythms and the repetition of motifs that remain as vestiges of orality while locking the patterns into word and text, which, for the scholar, allows for the trace and separation of the text into interpretable units. Each storyline presents the evolution of early Welsh society, hierarchically organized on the basis of patriarchal control. *The Mabinogion* opens then with both the male and the female components of society already in a state of transition; the motifs are redefined to give motivation to the male incursors and justification for suppressing the previous female-oriented society. For Kristeva, this would indicate the linking of the object (mother) with the abject male fear of control and castration by the object, unless some sort of control over the object can be effected[1]. The destruction of the other becomes the neurotic compulsion that fires the flames of phobia toward anything representative of the female. In a step by step process, this is exactly what occurs in a very logical progression throughout *The Mabinogion*: the denigration of female power and the celebration of paternity.

The usurpation of the birthing process, or the assumption of control over that process, is the first step necessary in establishing the dominance of the male element over a pre-existing female oriented society or culture. In order to control the process, however, knowledge of the male's role in biological conception had to be present. In the same way, once paternity had become established, protection of one's own property became the hallmark of a society building the male role in procreation into one of supremacy over the female. Once a child, especially a male heir, could be determined to belong to one man, then the mother had to be isolated from all other men as protection of the father's property. Without this important step, property and heirs could not be identified through the paternal line of descent. It would also follow that special prohibitions regarding the female's procreative role would arise, placing the female body into protective custody.

The Mabinogion presents the first branch in just such a conflict. Pwyll is offered the run of Arawn's kingdom as the two men seek to settle a conflict over property. Pwyll had set his dogs on a stag Arawn had killed; Pwyll has tried to steal Arawn's property. Pwyll's sense of ethics returns when he has the opportunity to sleep with Arawn's wife. But Pwyll remains chaste for his year in Arawn's stead; he does not touch Arawn's wife at all. Pwyll's chastity indicates the recognition of paternity; any child born from their union would not belong to Pwyll. The first branch begins then with an attempt by patriarchal culture (represented by Pwyll) to control the birthing process through abstention; this becomes the only power males would have that would insure that the choice of mother and the child born will belong to the father. It also indicates that Pwyll's culture is one that supports the acquisition of private property over that of communal ownership, represented by Arawn and his wife.

It is interesting to note that Arawn's wife is never named; she is only described in terms that would indicate her connection to the matri-focal culture.

She wears robes of "gold brocaded silk"[2]. The choice of color by the bard could indicate the peoples of the Early Bronze Age whose control over the process of metallurgy with gold and copper gave their ornamentations a cast of gold in the sunlight[3]. Pwyll's descent into Annwn, the Celtic underworld, also indicates his participation in rebirth ceremonies, common to the mythology of matri-focal cultures. The initiate sleeps for a determined period of time in what is considered a "mock death" in order to "feel reborn through the ceremonies"[4]. In this case, then, Pwyll's chastity would indicate his connection to Arawn's wife as one of son to ceremonial mother. This would give him the status of a convert into Arawn's society. Both interpretations are not mutually exclusive, however, most archaeological evidence indicates that when the patristic tribes first encountered the matri-focal groups, they exchanged members as a sign of good faith between the two systems[5]. Pwyll gains a new title from his exploits in the underworld, perhaps indicating the high regard and hopes for peace that initially existed between the two cultures of such different philosophies. It is later when the bonds of love are replaced with the bonds of power that it becomes clear that the two systems cannot coexist.

When Rhiannon marries Pwyll, she does so by her own choice and design; their son, Pryderi, is recognized as Pwyll's:

> And it came to his mind that in appearance he had never beheld a
> son and father so exceedingly alike as the boy to Pwyll Head of
> Annwn[6].

Two events are taking place in the story of Pryderi's birth: first, the acknowledgment of Pwyll as true parent of Pryderi; and second, the dissolution of female bonds between Rhiannon and the women who attend the birth. In terms of the first event, the names of the males are of importance; the name Pwyll means "Sense," Pryderi means "Care or Thought"[7]. The names indicate a growing consciousness on the part of the males. With the passing of every generation, they are becoming more conscious of themselves and their power. Between father and son, there is a movement from primal sense or instinct to thought, conscious and deliberate. Pryderi will be the first child of the new union between radically different social groups. He will also be the last of the successful heirs to hold the two groups together before the patristic group takes complete control away from the female aspect.

In terms of the second event, something else occurs. The dissolution of the bonds between the women who attend Pryderi's birth and Rhiannon indicate the separateness of the females within the society; instead of the strong tribal bonds within a matri-focused society, these women feel no loyalty toward each other; they would just as soon lie and perjure themselves than admit to their own incompetence (Women being incompetent about birth is a male fantasy anyway). The description of the birth itself becomes indicative of the women's motives:

> Before the end of that time came, a son was born to him, and in
> Arberth was he born. And on the night that he was born women
> were brought to watch the boy and his mother. The women fell
> asleep...[8].

Obviously, the boy is born to Pwyll, not to Rhiannon; as property and heir, he belongs to his father's family. That the women are "brought to watch" indicates the state of their passivity; they do not come out of a sense of sisterly concern, they come because they are brought; they don't seem to have a choice in the matter.

Rhiannon is removed from her husband's society when she is accused by the waiting women of eating her baby. Cannibalism is one of the oldest charges made against matri-focused groups; it probably existed in some form of sacrificial rites at some dim passage of human development from which the matristic groups evolved[9]. Psychologically, the charge made against Rhiannon is a charge made out of fear of being swallowed up by the maternal force. This episode also indicates the existence of purification rites for the female inherent in patriarchal religions:

> Fear of the archaic mother turns out to be essentially fear of her
> generative power. It is this power, a dreaded one, that patrilineal
> filiation has the burden of subduing. It is thus not surprising to see
> pollution rituals proliferating in societies where patrilineal power is
> poorly secured, as if the latter sought, by means of purification, a
> support against excessive matrilineality[10].

Branwen, in the second branch, also undergoes what could be interpreted as a purification rite after the birth of her son Gwern. Like Rhiannon, she is removed from the society of her husband and left to experience a daily "box on the ear[11]" from the butcher. Branwen, herself, has been objectified as a bartering tool of exogamy. She has been given over to Matholwich, leader of the Irish, because "'He seeks to align himself'"[12] with Bendigeidfran, Branwen's brother and king of the Island of the Mighty. Whereas "endogamy...implies in addition a specific filiation...of both parents at the same time"[13], exogamy implies filiation with the paternal tribe. Hence, the heir Gwern becomes the property of the Irish, not a part of Branwen's line of descent. Efnisien, brother to Bendigeidfran by matri-lineal descent, is outraged at the trade and insult of his sister and destroys Gwern in an effort to re-establish control over those lines. Branwen almost gets lost amid the fighting warriors from both sides. She has been reduced to pawn in a game between greater and stronger male powers, but she herself as a Goddess figure is impotent.

By the third branch, the symbolism of the pregnant mouse indicates the denigration and minimization of the female biological function of birth as well as the female herself. Control of her fate is now a battle between the men and the religious clerics of the story. As a mouse, she is small enough to be hidden easily; she is also silent, with no voice to express her outrage, neither can she protect herself from the giant who holds her captive. There is also a sense that control of agriculture, a specifically female domain of prehistory, has also passed into male hands as Manawydan teaches himself the art of husbandry (the word itself is indicative of its function). And as the oldest primitive religious beliefs from anywhere in the world believed in the female Mother Earth, Manawydan's farming symbolizes a taming or domestication of the earth herself to masculine control and manipulation.

This manipulation is further developed in the fourth and final branch of *The Mabinogion* as Math and Gwydion create a woman (Blodeuedd) completely out of vegetable matter[14]. This is preceded by Aranrhod's complete denial of maternity and her ignorance about pregnancy. Control over the birthing process is in the hands of the patriarchy; it conceives, it births, and it parents without the maternal presence or influence. The establishment of patri-lineal descent is complete because the male is the only recognized parent of the offspring; the female becomes superfluous to the process. Even the hero Llew Llau Gyffes gestates at the foot of Gwydion's bed[15] instead of the maternal womb. The male characters take on the maternal role by assuming maternal characteristics. It is at this point that the Tierisias motif presented in the fourth branch takes on such a distinctive role in patriarchal myth.

Tierisias, the female-male sage of Greek mythology, embodies one of the stages of male usurpation of the birthing process through his exchange of sexual identities. His character is unique and original to the patriarchal myth; he changes sex to uncover and understand "the reality from both sides that each sex experiences shadow like from its own side[16]. Tierisias emerges from his experience with the female secrets regarding sex. Both Gwydion and Gilfaethwy undergo the same sex-shifting, each becoming female and male and producing offspring, as punishment for the rape of Math's maiden. It is after this experience that Gwydion then assumes the role of both father and mother to Aranrhod's children. Male birthing of offspring, like that of Zeus' in Greek mythology and the assumption of the female Shekinah by the male Elohim in Hebrew mythology, now becomes possible.

The symbolism of the animals Gwydion and Gilfaethwy become in their sex-shifting indicates the assumption of control by the male element over the mythic past. The order the animals appear in the text (stag, pig, wolf) is their chronological order of their individual worship in prehistory, the most ancient animal worshipped being the stag, the most recent being the wolf[17]. The male element takes control of the present by assuming control over the past and, in effect, rewriting ancient history into male terms.

This rewriting continues as rank and power are reordered to indicate the ascension of male superiority and the declination of the female aspect. Throughout *The Mabinogion*, the author records various feasts which, through the actual seating of the participants, methodically eliminate the female from the seat of societal power and cultural control. The purposes of the feasts vary slightly, but as acts of sharing food with those with whom alliances are to be sanctified, these purposes finally abstract the female as the food being consumed.

In the first branch, the feast seating moves from Rhiannon as participant to Pryderi as central and "above"[18] his parents or his heritage. In the second branch, Matholwch assumes Branwen's position; she is reduced to mere dinner companion[19]. By the third branch, the order the crafts and the order of the Christian clerics replace the feasts; the patriarchal structure is in place by this time; there is no need to share food for alliances. In the fourth branch, the only feast recorded is between Gwydion, as false bard, and Pryderi, the last representative of the initial union of the two cultures. The female aspect has been reduced to ancient history: "pleasant tales and story-telling"[20] about the mythic past. The feast itself is now open to treachery and deceit, no more an emblem of honor between peoples.

Motherhood (female fecundity) also goes through a process of denigration and separation from the biological function. There is a decided movement from fecundity to sterility and a maternal denial of complicity in the process of human creation. The pollution and purification rites inherent in the calumniated wife motif indicate punishment of the female for her ability to give birth:

> such a force is rooted, historically (in the history of religions) and
> subjectively...in the cathexsis of maternal function -- mother,
> woman, reproduction. [It] consists in subordinating maternal power
> (whether historical or phantasmatic, natural or reproductive) to
> symbolic order as pure logical order regulating social
> performance[21].

Rhiannon is the first wife to undergo such punishment. Her story indicates the fragmentation of the female community and the loss of authority in raising her child. The introduction of foster parentage is indicative of the transition between the two cultures. Branwen, too, is punished after the birth of Gwern. She also is involved with losing her child as her heir and reinforcing the relatively new lines of patri-lineal descent. By the third branch, Manawydan's attempt to overcome the wasteland becomes symbolic of the male's level of control rising over the fecund earth. The pregnant mouse represents the debasement of the female function of birth as an animal function devoid of the higher levels of human existence. With the fourth branch, male control over motherhood is complete; Aranrhod denies any maternal culpability related to the birth process. She refuses to mother and must be tricked by Gwydion into giving her son his name and his weapons. Blodeuedd represents the sterility motherhood has now undergone; as a vegetable creature, she lacks the blood that would allow her to be a mother, not to mention being human.

This denigration allows for the female to become the target for the outrages of sacrifice and death inherent in masculine power and control. Rhiannon is transformed from Goddess to beast of burden. Efnisien's maiming of the horses becomes editorial comment on the exchange of Branwen in marriage like some kind of commodity. By the third branch, rape has become the bane of any unprotected female. The Persephone motif introduced with the disappearance of Rhiannon and Pryderi is placed under masculine control. Even Blodeuedd's fate is one of living death; she is sentenced to assume the guise of an owl, once an honored creature in the matriarchal pantheon, but here it has been transformed to just a night bird living off the carrion of the fields.

The reconstituted use of female symbolism, therefore, becomes an arrest in female development and a fragmentation of the female aspect under the assumption of societal control by the masculine element. The use of the hunt motif in this regard indicates the struggle of the male against the female. The animals of the hunt and the females themselves become interchangeable as the struggle between the two cultures closes in for the kill. The initial hunt that begins the first branch indicates the presence of personal property in regard to the female. In the second branch, Branwen's brothers actually go on a hunt for their sister. The white boar (symbol of the Goddess) hunted by Pryderi captures him in a cycle of death and rebirth. He must be redeemed by an exchange of a pregnant mouse the bishop is hunting for. Blodeuedd's lover hunts for a stag; he is an enemy of the already established male order. Blodeuedd, as the last female figure in *The Mabinogion*, becomes the symbol of the reconstituted, and developmentally arrested, female: the eternal and sterile virgin.

Along with denying the maternal, or life-giving, powers of the Goddess, the text of *The Mabinogion* also denies her death and rebirth aspect. According to matristic philosophy, one dies in order to be reborn through the Goddess. The ending of the mythology of rebirth through the female culminates in a masculine control of that process. Pwyll dies an unremarkably human death, being only a convert of the matristic system. Branwen, too, suffers the fate of human death with no indication of rebirth. Efnisien destroys the cauldron of rebirth in a heroic attempt to destroy that which would have only benefited the new power system. Pryderi and Rhiannon's apparent disappearance is controlled by the actions of a human male in conjunction with the religious clerics, denoting an exchange of the power of rebirth into Christian hands. The Persephone motif introduced through Rhiannon's disappearance into the mist does not end when the Goddess redeems the dead, but when Manawydan redeems them. The story of Llew Llau Gyffes indicates the complete assumption of rebirth by the masculine communal savior.

When Gwydion discovers the "sow feeding on rotten flesh and maggots"[22], he is actually observing the goddess feasting on the flesh of the sacrificed: "in another connection consuming the leavings of a sacrifice can also be the cause of a series of good rebirths and can even lead to finding salvation"[23]. But Gwydion interrupts the process (as he did with the process of procreation) by removing the sacrificed eagle and performing the rites of rebirth himself. In fact, Llew Llau Gyffes is a "kind of Celtic Mercury"[24] and, as such, would be the new designated "conductor of souls to the afterworld"[25]. It is now through Llew Llau Gyffes that rebirth becomes possible.

And so the text of *The Mabinogion* moves through to its ultimate conclusion: the patristic assumption of societal and religious control from the matri-focused community. By suppressing, denigrating, and dehumanizing the female aspect, the patriarchal social structure can stand alone in control of the society. The Christian cleric has now assumed the primacy of the male over the female processes of human life complete with the deification and resurrection of the male deity. This becomes inherent in the fact that it is the cleric who is recording the myth, and so, assumes the voice of history and authority while indicating that same authority for the written word:

> But the frame of reference of this written literature was still the multifarious oral tradition which, unlike its written offshoot, was at the disposal of all and enjoyed free passage from province to province and from class to class. Consequently, the monastic redactor could shape the phrasing of his narrative in the sure knowledge that his readers (or auditors) would be sensitive to the vast and flexible range of connotations which existed in its full variety and vitality only within the oral tradition[26].

The text of *The Mabinogion* presents a clear picture of the denigration of female consciousness that leaves control over the life processes to the male. As other texts of patriarchal origins indicate, this is the first step on the road to established authority. *The Mabinogion's* structuring of the female motif indicates the step by step process inherent in dismantling one system in favor of setting up another. By reducing women to property, by assuming control of the birthing process, by denigrating the female in social affairs, and finally by assuming control over death and rebirth, the patriarchal social system comes into full enforcement with the complete absorption of the matristic culture. The revised female consciousness becomes one without power, without voice, and without memory:

> It will then fall upon analysis to give back a memory, hence a language, to unnamable states of fear, while emphasizing the former, which make up what is most unapproachable in the unconscious[27].

It will also fall upon women to give back a memory of lost mothers and sisters in texts that still await decoding, that still await the chance for liberation from the word that encases them. The process of revising female consciousness once again becomes the purpose of such work, the purpose of drying the tears of Rhiannon.

[1]Kristeva, Julia. *Powers of Horror: An Essay on Abjection*. (New York: Columbia University Press, 1982.) 33.

[2]Jones, Gwyn and Thomas, eds. *The Mabinogion*. (London: Guernsey Press, 1986.) 5.

[3]Clark, Grahame. *Prehistoric England*. (London: B. T. Batesford, 1945.) 43.

[4]Johnson, Buffie. *Lady of the Beasts*. (San Francisco: Harper and Row, 1988.) 92.

[5]French, Marilyn. *Beyond Power: On Women, Men and Morals*. (New York: Summit Books, 1985.) 76.

[6]Jones 21.

[7]Jones 23.

[8]Jones 18.

[9]Campbell, Joseph. *The Masks of God: Primitive Mythology*. (New York: Penguin Books, 1987.) 170.

[10]Kristeva 77.

[11]Jones 32.

[12]Jones 26.

[13]Kristeva 79.

[14]Jones 68.

[15]Jones 64.

[16]Campbell, Joseph. *The Masks of God: Occidental Mythology*. (New York: Penguin Books, 1982.) 171.

[17]Walker, Barbara G. *The Woman's Dictionary of Symbols and Sacred Objects*. (San Francisco: Harper and Row, 1988.) 360.

[18]Jones 22.

[19]Jones 26.

[20]Jones 57.

[21]Kristeva 91.

[22]Jones 72.

[23]Kristeva 76.

[24]Ross 197.

[25]Campbell, Joseph. *The Hero With a Thousand Faces*. (Princeton: Princeton University Press, 1949.) 72.

[26]MacCana, Proinsias. "Mythology in Early Irish Literature." in *The Celtic Consciousnss*. ed. Robert O'Driscoll. (New York: George Braziller, 1982.) 145.

[27]Kristeva 37.

Growing Flowers of Life Everlasting:
Feminist Archetypal Theory and Ellen Glasgow's *Barren Ground*

A woman's life is hard in its own way, as women have always known and men have rarely understood.

-Ellen Moers

So writes Ellen Moers in her ground breaking analysis about women writers, *Literary Women*, which virtually ignores Ellen Glasgow's work as a feminist writer. And yet, *Barren Ground* epitomizes Moer's comment about a woman's life and presents the development of its central character, Dorinda Oakley, as an archetypal questor searching for self and personal autonomy. Written in 1925, *Barren Ground* also marks the passage of its author into full writing maturity; about the novel, Glasgow commented, "'it is the best book I have written'" and it "remained her favorite among her nineteen published novels"[1]. Perhaps this is due to the fact that *Barren Ground* in many ways parallels the author's own life and experiences growing up in rural Virginia and coming to terms with being a woman and searching for a higher purpose in her existence.

Glasgow presents Dorinda as an archetypal hero achieving personal and psychological development as she passes through the archetypal female life stages of virgin, mother, and crone, marked by the divisions of the novel as "Broomsedge", "Pine", and "Life-Everlasting"[2]. From my own theorhetical background in feminist archetypal theory, grounded in the work of Annis Pratt, Estella Lauter and Carol Schreieir Rupprecht, and Sylvia Brinton Perera among others, it is my contention that the three life stages of virgin, mother, crone, represent the adventure quest for woman's self actualization initially expressed in mythology as the archetype of the ancient goddess and the stories of her own personal development[3]. Each stage carries its own unique psychological markers that enable a woman's movement toward self acceptance and personal autonomy. The pattern can be traced in almost every novel of development written by women for women. In this case, I shall apply the basics of my theory to Glasgow's hero, Dorinda, as she moves from ignorance to knowledge, from lack of control to personal autonomy, from detachment from her patristic heritage to a full embrace of her female inheritance.

This development of the female hero parallels the development of the male hero in classical tragedy, but includes a significant difference. The female hero, like the male, is a universal figure who endures a descent in search of knowledge; usually, a choral presence and a prophet-seer try to help the hero achieve some kind of understanding of her fate and destiny. The difference between the male and female heroes is that the male usually dies (Oedipus, Hamlet) or is condemned to a lifetime of wandering (Adam, Cain) while the female hero learns and accepts life-long endurance (Demeter, Inanna, Linda Loman in "Death of a Salesman", Jane Eyre, Janie in *Their Eyes Were Watching God*, Deb in *Life in the Iron Mills*, Eva in "Tell Me a Riddle").

In *Barren Ground*, all of these characteristics appear. The novel is set in a poor, rural county of Virginia which Glasgow identifies as "Queen Elizabeth"[4], beginning the novel's rich associations with female archetypes. At this point in time, Dorinda is a young woman of twenty who is searching for adventure and purpose as she stares out of the window at Pedlar's Mill, "her attitude in its stillness, gave an impression of arrested flight, as if she were running toward life"[5]. Glasgow insists that Dorinda is "truly a universal figure"[6] who is beginning her quest amid the pervading image of the broomsedge which personifies her youthful passion. The tone at the beginning of the novel emphasizes the tragic elements through the entire novel: "Most of the crucial scenes in the book... take place against the broomsedge in the autumn and establish an autumnal meloncholy as the dominating mood of the novel"[7]. Dorinda experiences a fall from grace in her thwarted love affair, a failed hieros gamos, with Jason Graylock, a fall so encompassing that Dorinda spends the rest of her life trying to mitigate it. Her development and personal growth become part of the pattern of the universal woman and the tragedy of mortal life; the end of the novel provides the appropriate catharsis for the audience that tragedy must supply in order to be effectual.

The prophet-seer, another characteristic apparent in all tales of tragedy, is represented in the character of Nathan Pedlar, owner of the Mill and eventual husband to Dorinda. Glasgow writes from her own religious background, providing Biblical touchstones for her readers (Dorinda's father reminds her of John the Baptist, the family's horses are named Dan and Beersheba). In this case, the name of Nathan recalls the Biblical story of the prophet Nathan who moves King David to condemn himself by presenting to the king a parable about a poor man's pet ewe lamb who, "'was unto him as a daughter'" (II Samuel 12:3). The ewe is stolen to provide food for a rich man's table. David becomes incensed about the crime, declaring "'As the Lord liveth, the man that had done this deserveth to die; and he shall restore the lamb forfeited, because he did this thing, and because he had no pity'" (II Samuel 12:5). Nathan then declares that David is himself the rich man who stole the ewe (Bathsheba) from the poor warrior Uriah. David repents, but cannot free himself from the punitive consequences of his actions. Nathan tells him "'Behold, I will raise up an evil against you out of your own house, and I will take thy wives before thine eyes, and give them unto thy neighbor'"; he goes on to say, "'the child that is born to thee [from David's adultery] shall surely die'" (II Samuel 12:11-14). It is through Nathan's influence as a prophet that Solomon, son of Bathsheba rather than the son of David's choice, becomes the next king of Israel.

With this touchstone in mind, it is clear to see what Glasgow intends in working out the fates of Jason (as David) and Dorinda (as Bathsheba). Nathan Pedlar, as prophetic voice, not only foresees the end of Jason and the sale of his farm Five Oaks, but Nathan is also instrumental in placing Five Oaks into Dorinda's hands. On the day of Dorinda and Nathan's wedding, Geneva (Jason's now deranged wife) appears on the road before them, insane and incoherent, her downfall being Jason's drinking and the infertility of their marriage, the Biblical prophecy ringing true. It is also interesting to note that in the novel, nobody believes Geneva's ravings about Jason killing (drowning) their first-born. As readers, we too are led to write off Geneva's charges as crazy and insane. But what if Geneva is telling the truth?

Nathan Pedlar is an agricultural visionary in this sleepy, rural county, but not too many people take him seriously during his lifetime either. Although he helps Dorinda pioneer new farming techniques, it is not until after his death that he is given the respect and admiration of the people of the county. The grave marker erected for him gives Nathan the status of prophet in death as he was in life: "Every soldier who went from Pedlar's Mill was reminded by fire-breathing orators that the heroes of war must be worthy of the hero of peace. Every appeal from the Red Cross in this county bore his name as an ornament. As time went on this legend... gathered a patina of tradition as a tombstone gathers moss"[8], "'Then future generations will remember his heroism'"[9]. Nathan's death brings a "foretaste of spring"[10]; Dorinda finally realizes that Nathan had "filled the aching void in her life"[11], and had provided "a romantic background for her life"[12].

The traditional Greek chorus is presented alternately by three different elements: Old Matthew Fairlamb, the black farm workers, and the land itself. Old Matthew, as a "one man tragic chorus"[13] representing time and wisdom, "possesses an oracular, cynical wisdom"[14]. He directs Dorinda to "'Put yo' heart in the land. The land is the only thing that will stay by you'"[15]; his remark comes back as an almost lyrical refrain to Dorinda in her later years as she recognizes her "permanent self" in a "living communion with the earth under her feet"[16]. A sentiment that will become the mainstay for Margaret Mitchell's hero Scarlet in *Gone With The Wind*, written soon after *Barren Ground*. The black farm workers are a constant presence in the novel, and Glasgow uses them to reflect and oppose Dorinda's own feelings and determination. After Nathan's death, they appear again in a "loud disorganization" of "lamenting the dead"[17]. But it is the land itself, the literal barren ground (the title of the novel being repeated several times in the book), which constitutes the strongest choral presence and "frequently turns out to be a manifestation of the psyche"[18], reflecting Dorinda's sensual passions that move from wasteland motif to fertility and abundance. Because she works with the land, because she acknowledges the "inescapable influence of soil upon soul"[19], Dorinda eventually rises victorious with nature by means of her feelings of independance and autonomy:

> In literature dealing with the single woman...authors seem to be clearing out a new space that is in actuality an old, or archetypal landscape of the psyche, a place that, essentially apatriarchal, contains the once-forgotten possibilities of personal development. Rekindling old images, buried archetypes, and discarded choices, such fiction brings its heroes through quests toward personal transformations or rebirth[20].

In contrast to Dorinda, Jason allows himself to be defeated by his internal passions; he ignores his own fate, and because of this, he is covered in broomsedge[21] and is eventually swallowed up by the land in death. As Old Matthew says, "'he's got everything you want in a man except the one quality that counts with the land'"[22].

Within this atmosphere of Greek tragedy, Glasgow places her hero Dorinda. And because this is a novel of female development, Glasgow demonstrates the circularity of woman's heritage which Glasgow calls an "enchanted circle"[23] and woman's ties to the "trivial"[24], physical life. In the depiction of Rose Emily's daughters playing at funeral games with their dolls, which foreshadows their mother's death as well as other funerals that will follow in progression, Glasgow emphasizes the woman's connection with the acceptance of the mortality of human life indocrinated into girls as young as Rose Emily's daughters.

"Broomsedge," the first part of the novel, shows Dorinda as the young virgin with an "April charm and a vital, romantic spirit"[25] encountering Eros in the guise of Jason and in her own inexperienced feelings of passion. Dorinda believes this to be her hieros gamos, the great love of her life. But Jason falls far short of a deserving lover. He is weak and vain and self centered about his own ambitions. He takes advantage of Dorinda's love instead of loving her back equally. In the green world of spring, love blossoms; in the heat of the summer, passions grow, but this particular summer is marked by drought, foreshadowing the the blighted growth within Dorinda's own body. Her inexperience in love opens a "virgin wilderness of mystery and terror"[26] that culminates in Jason's betrayal of their engagement. In confronting Jason's deceit and in seeking the truth for herself, she descends into an "ultimate darkness. There was an abyss around her...She lay flat in this vacancy"[27]. This descent is carried on to New York where Dorinda attempts to rebuild her life after her miscarriage. It is here she encounters the concert music that acts as a "guide leading her down into her buried self, where she makes a decision to return to the land"[28].

      In the virgin aspect of a woman's life, there is an attempt by the hero to separate from her mother and her mother's heritage in order to define her own existence, to make her own choices. When Dorinda tries to talk with her mother about love and its significance for women, her mother replies, "'if it's a woman's nature to take it too hard, it's just as much the nature of man to take it too easy...It's just the struggle to get away from things as they are'"[29]. Dorinda rejects this rationalization, insisting to herself that for her, love will be different. For her mother, as well as for Glasgow's generation, "mating seems to equal identity for the young woman"[30]; Dorinda wants more than just this definition for herself, as did Glasgow. As an "archetype of the liberated woman"[31] liberated from both the unwanted pregnancy and from initial financial need, Dorinda realizes she must return to Old Farm and create for herself a personal legacy as well as a reclamation of the female heritage she initially rejected. When she gets the news of her father's critical illness, she returns home, initiating the second phase of her development -- the mother phase -- marked by the second division of the novel entitled "Pine."

      In this section, Dorinda becomes parent to her parents and mother to Old Farm. On her return, Nathan has painted his store red, a symbolic color of the maternal blood of life and birth[32]. She begins the slow process of land reclamation and rebuilding with the money she has borrowed from her friends in New York. She enters the stage of mother in psychological development by giving herself to a greater purpose: "kinship with the land"[33]. Her "diffused maternal spirit"[34] is given "To protect, to lift up, rebuild and restore, these impulses formed the deepest obligation that nature could feel"[35]; "she had projected all her fertility into the land"[36] in an attempt to save what her father as "weakened progeny"[37] was unable to salvage. The pine tree that her father transfixed upon at his death is contrasted with the dream in which Dorinda sees the memory of Jason as unwieldy thistle to be plowed under. The pine stands over the small family cemetary, indicating that from death comes life, and from life comes death; the circularity of the process becomes crystallized for Dorinda as well as for her mother: "'I reckon it's a heathenish way to think about things...but I can't help thinking there's a heap of comfort in it'"[38]. The strength of Dorinda's own character is derived from her mother who, nearing death, speaks of returning to her own green world of her past and her own dreams of being a missionary, redeeming the "heathen"[39] of Africa with Christian salvation.

      In this stage of development, Dorinda works as hard as any man, dresses in men's clothing, immerses herself in the man's world of farming. When she makes a success of it all, she buys new dresses and returns to church not only a victor, but a female victor. She has reconciled the two worlds of the masculine and the feminine in finding a definition and acceptance of self as well as a tolerance over love[40] in her marriage with Nathan. With her acquisition of Jason's run-down Five Oaks, she enters her final stage, and the novel's final division, of crone and of "Life-Everlasting."

In this section, all the lessons of her life become clear to her now. Her mastery of the agricultural processes is achieved through the clearing of the land of Five Oaks; "as if the fire and smoke were clearing her life of its illusions"[41]. She has developed a "philosophy of acquiescence"[42] that allows her to accept her life and her self: "Mastery of the impersonal powers of nature is assured only when mastery of the self is complete"[43]. She becomes the crone of wisdom as well as the crone of prophecy; "'Perhaps at fifty I shall be rid of [the illusions] forever'"[44].

In leading up to the episode of Nathan's death, Glasgow sets the scene and the tone by using the words "ghostly images"[45], "shrouded"[46], "dead and buried"[47], "Judgement Day"[48] which reflect Dorinda's new phase of development as crone, harbinger of death and human mortality. When Nathan is late returning home, Dorinda has premonitions about his death:

>Presently, notwithstanding her effort to minimize the cause for alarm, she became aware that anxiety was stealing over her as if it emanated from her surroundings. She felt it first in the creeping sensation which ran like spiders over her flesh; then in an almost imperceptible twitching of her muscles; and at last in a delicate vibration of her nerves, as if a message were passing over electric wires in her body. Then, suddenly, the fear mounted to her brain, and she found herself listening like John Abner for the crunching of wheels in the snow...[49].
>A chill passed down Dorinda's spine, but she was unaware of the cause that produced it, and her mind was vacant of thought. Then, while the wagon jolted up the slope, some meaningless words darted into her consciousness. "Something has happened. I feel that something has happened"[50].

Before the men at the station could tell her, Dorinda tells them that Nathan is dead[51]. The appearence of Elisha's "'ole grey mare'"[52] and of Dorinda's "Snowbird, her big white horse with a flowing mane and the plaited tail which had never been docked"[53] further Dorinda's association with the mythological night-mare ridden by the crone in her guise as harbinger of death. The years of pine give way to the years of life-everlasting, placing Dorinda in the continuum of life: "The rebirth journey takes the hero beyond social boundaries and back again, its goal the renewel of society"[54]. When Dorinda dresses for Nathan's funeral, she puts in the "crape veil which has been worn by two generations of widows"[55] which inexorably connects Dorinda to the female heritage she once denied, but which now provides her with the wisdom of a life spent in service to the land and in satisfaction with her work: "nature lifts Dorinda beyond humanity into consciousness of a transcendant Power"[56]. It is life on her own terms with an "aspect of eternity"[57].

Dorinda also achieves a part of her mother's dream to bring salvation to the heathen blacks in the "fallen tropical Eden"[58] of Africa, by helping the poor black families who surround her woman-made Eden of Old Farm. She educates her friend Fluvanna, teaches her farm workers discipline and fulfillment through hard work, and only hires black women as milkers "inspired by a firm though illogical belief in their superior neatness"[59]. Dorinda has entered the community of women as a leader and as a compatriot; Mrs. Garlick shares her widow's bonnet with Dorinda, "'she can't wear it herself until she loses John'"[60]. Notice the word "until"; this is a special community of women one is initiated into by the seemingly inevitable loss of a husband, but one that is strengthened by its numbers of women members.

As crone, Dorinda enters the larger world when the war breaks out, a war "won by the help of the farmers"[61]. The war to end all wars becomes the vehicle for Dorinda to bring salvation on her own terms to the entire world through her farming success:

> If the purpose of the novel of development is to integrate the
> individual into her society, its generic function is frequently aborted
> by society's unwillingness to assimilate her. The older woman hero,
> in contrast, has been 'through all that,' her goal is to integrate
> herself with herself and not with a society she has found inimical to
> her desires[62].

When Dorinda offers to take the dying Jason in, she acts as his guide into the nether regions of death by providing him with the tranquil surroundings and the peace of mind necessary for his passage. She realizes that because "he had lost all connections to his surroundings"[63], he himself is lost. By maintaining and building her ties with the past, she has been able to achieve a continuum of purpose and life everlasting. The one phrase that is echoed over and over again is Dorinda's line "'through with all that'" that reverberates seven times in the novel as Dorinda passes through her stages of development, subconsciously mimicking perhaps the seven gates the Sumerian Goddess Inanna must pass through to meet her other self/sister, Ereshkigal. But in its final presentation, once Nathan is gone and Jason is gone and she has provided for the land's passing into the next generation of her step-son John Abner, Dorinda speaks the final line of the novel with emphasis, maturity, and pride, "'I am thankful to be finished with all that'"[64]. No more bitterness, no more recriminations of self or others, just a simple but noble acceptance of life, of self, and of purpose.

Ellen Glasgow was raised in rural Virginia, suffered an ill-fated love affair, distained sexual intimacy, and remained single all of her life. *Barren Ground*, written when she was fifty-two, is as much as an exploration of the author's own past as it is Dorinda's. Glasgow felt that *Barren Ground* was "'the truest novel ever written'; 'true to...life and to the inevitable change and fall of the years. The book deserves to live. It is a perfectly honest interpretation of experience, without illusion, without evasion'"[65]. Although Glasgow achieved a fair amount of critical acclaim in her lifetime, her work has generally not received more than passing references in feminist scholarship even though her writing basically defined Southern regionalism for the male canonical writers who would follow her, Allen Tate, Stark Young, Robert Penn Warren, and especially William Faulkner:

> Not surprisingly, she was ascendant while Faulkner struggled in
> relative obscurity, but as his reputation rose mightily, hers fell with
> startling rapidity[66].

About twelve years after the appearance of *Barren Ground*, Margaret Mitchell's *Gone With the Wind* capitalized on the female connection between "soil and soul" with her protagonist Scarlet O'Hara, a connection first pioneered by Ellen Glasgow. During the late thirties, Edith Summers Kelly wrote *Weeds*, again a novel dealing with the female inheritance of endurance and personal autonomy in relationship to the land and to life.

With *Barren Ground*, Glasgow does more than "punish an unsuitable mate"[67], or teach that "there is nothing beyond the earth"[68]; in Glasgow's relationship with Dorinda, she does not emerge "embittered", "cynical", "frustrated", or "pathetic"[69]; and Dorinda's vein of iron is more than her "Presbyterian conscience"[70]. Ellen Glasgow presents a novel of development that spans a woman's lifetime, a woman who finds her purpose and her autonomy with the land, a woman who is acutely aware of the human struggle to accept subservience to Nature; the male tragedy is that he cannot; the woman's tragedy is that she already has, alone.

There is ample material in Glasgow's writings for feminist scholars to explore. Her use of woman as tragic hero on the quest for self actualization embodies the twentieth century's involvement with novels of personal development. Her work with regionalism raised the genre to an art form. We have been amiss in neglecting Ellen Glasgow, but to paraphrase the author's own words, where human beings have failed her, her own heroic legend will satisfy.

---

[1]Scura, Dorothy McInnis. "*Barren Ground*: Ellen Glasgow's Critical Arrival." in *Mississippi Quarterly*. 32.4 (Fall, 1979) 550.
[2]Glasgow, Ellen. *Barren Ground*. (New York: Coubleday, 1925.) 1, 195, 395.
[3]For a complete expanation of my therory regarding female development, please refer to my book, *Life Stages of Woman's Heroic Journey*. (New York: Edwin Mellen Press, 1991.)

[4]Glasgow 5.
[5]Glasgow 3.
[6]Santas, Joan Foster. *Ellen Glasgow's American Dream*. (Charlottesville: University Press of Virginia, 1965.) 138.
[7]McDowell, Frederick P. W. *Ellen Glasgow and the Ironic Art of Ficton*. (Madison: University of Wisconsin Press, 1960.) 252.
[8]Glasgow 457.
[9]Glasgow 441.
[10]Glasgow 443.
[11]Glasgow 456
[12]Glasgow 457.
[13]McDowell 147.
[14]McDowell 157.
[15]Glasgow 323.
[16]Glasgow 509
[17]Glasgow 433-34
[18]Raper, Julius Rowan. *From the Sunken Garden: The Fiction of Ellen Glasgow: 1916-1945.* (Baton Rouge: Louisiana State University Press, 1980.) 79.
[19]McDowell 147.
[20]Pratt, Annis. *Archetypal Patterns in Women's Fiction*. (Bloomington: Indiana University Press, 1981.) 127.
[21]Glasgow 389, 453.
[22]Glasgow 133.
[23]Glasgow 33.
[24]Glasgow 23.
[25]Santas 151.
[26]Glasgow 69.
[27]Glasgow 156.
[28]Pratt 20.
[29]Glasgow 103.
[30]Wagner, Linda W. "*Barren Ground's* Vein of Iron: Dorinda Oakley and Some Concepts of the Heroine in 1925. " in *Mississippi Quarterly*. 32.4 (Fall, 1979) 555.
[31]Frazee, Monique Parent. "Ellen Glasgow as Feminist." in *Centennial Essays*. ed. M. Thomas Inge. (Charlottesville: University Press of Virginia, 1976.) 181.
[32]Glasgow 252.
[33]Glasgow 299.
[34]Glasgow 361.
[35]Glasgow 341.
[36]Raper 97.
[37]Santas 139.
[38]Glasgow 297.
[39]Glasgow 334.
[40]Glasgow 376.
[41]Glasgow 401.
[42]Glasgow 398.
[43]McDowell 151
[44]Glasgow 401.
[45]Glasgow 405.

[46]Glasgow 416.
[47]Glasgow 426.
[48]Glasgow 421.
[49]Glasgow 419.
[50]Glasgow 429.
[51]Glasgow 431.
[52]Glasgow 423.
[53]Glasgow 450.
[54]Pratt 137.
[55]Glasgow 435.
[56]McDowell 153.
[57]McDowell 158.
[58]Bond, Tonette L. "Pastoral Transformations in *Barren Ground*." in *Mississippi Quarterly*. 32.4 (Fall, 1979). 592.
[59]Glasgow 408.
[60]Glasgow 436.
[61]Glasgow 446.
[62]Pratt 136.
[63]Glasgow 495.
[64]Glasgow 511.
[65]Wagner 559.
[66]Wittenberg, Judith B. "The Critical Fortunes of *Barren Ground*." in *Mississippi Quarterly*. 32.4 (Fall, 1979). 592.
[67]Pratt 19.
[68]Raper 225.
[69]Gobold Jr., E. Stanley. *Ellen Glasgow and the World Within*. (Baton Rouge: Louisiana State University Press, 1972.) 137.
[70]Raper 82.

Sovereignty of Self:
Christina Rossetti's *Speaking Likenesses*

Who I was I am, who I am I must be for ever and ever...I may loathe myself, or be amazed at myself, But I cannot unself myself for ever and ever.

- Christina Rossetti

Representing the self in various bifurcations and fragmentations is a dominant theme in Christina Rossetti's writings. Many of her poems deal with the divided self, the self in conflict with societal norms, or the integration of the self into wholeness. It is through this theme that Rossetti develops an acceptance of her own poetic destiny and a philosophy of female survival in a world that insisted on feminine conformation and compliance. Lines of this philosophy can be gleaned throughout her poetry, but the unified whole of the female experience with the self can be found in Rossetti's children's book *Speaking Likenesses*. It is through this book that Christina Rossetti imparts a learning text for young Victorian girls on personal development and self fulfillment. But its symbolism tells as much about Rossetti's own life as it does about the female heroes presented; through her own experience, Rossetti frames a psychological tale of female development that becomes less a guidebook for manners and more a study of the process of identification for the female individual.

Biography, that "old illusion" as Virginia Woolf calls it, doesn't offer us very much information on the personal Rossetti. She remained separate and aloof from her society, choosing a life alone dedicated to her talents rather than a life of marriage and children. The only public work she did was with the Magdalen Home for Fallen Women from 1860 to 1870[1]. Rossetti maintained close relationships with her siblings, but, more importantly, remained devoted to her mother and her elder aunts all through her life. Otherwise, writing was her passion.

All the Rossetti children were quite precocious, especially Christina, whose high spirits and artistic temperament denoted a child of unique sensibilities. The gardens of the family home were filled with the nature that taught Christina about the mutability of earthly life and provided her with the vegetative poetic images that would fill her writing for years to come. Christina balanced this temporal nature with a deep and abiding spirituality which remained her strength to the end of her life. Although her brothers did not share in her religiosity, William Michael and Dante Gabriel each portrayed her as saintly and angelic, hoping to add to the iconography of her reputation[2]. If she wasn't to be in this world, then they would insure her reputation in the next. During her life, Dante Gabriel portrayed her in his paintings as the Virgin Mary and as Jesus paintings; William Michael rewrote and reedited various poems of Christina's after her death. Their sense of fraternal protectiveness about their sister is the source of many of the erroneous assumptions about Christina that have been inherited by the modern reader.

There are about as many misconceptions about *Speaking Likenesses* as there are about its author. Usually referred to as minor at best, unimportant at worst, *Speaking Likenesses* has never had an important critical approach. Most critics refer to it as a poor imitation of Lewis Carroll's Alice stories[3]. Others prefer to see it as a failure in terms of its market value. Originally titled *Nowhere,* *Speaking Likenesses* was written with a commercial intent on the part of Rossetti; she described it as "'three short stories in a framework.'"[4] She changed the title with her realization that "' my small heroines perpetually encounter 'speaking' (literally 'speaking') likenesses or embodiments of themselves or their faults. I think the title boasts of some point and neatness.'"[5] It appeared on the shelves in 1874, and disappeared almost as quickly:

> The children for whom she wrote *Speaking Likenesses,* with their
> instinctive and unanswerable wisdom, consigned it to oblivion long
> ago, and only the scholar or the curiosity-seeker exhumes it today[6].

But there is another element to consider with *Speaking Likenesses:* there isn't any other work of Rossetti's that has been as historically ignored as this one slim volume. Admittedly, not everything written by a gifted author can enjoy the same rank as other, already accepted works, but does *Speaking Likenesses* deserve to be consigned as a curiosity? Rossetti herself, known for her sense of particularity in regards to the balance and exactitude of her work, was quite pleased with the children's book upon its completion. Is there something about *Speaking Likenesses* that has eluded scholars who have not traditionally thought it worthy enough to include in any complete study on Rossetti's work? Even though *Speaking Likenesses* may never achieve the same status and regard as *Goblin Market,* it does demonstrate the evolution of female development from dependent child to independent individualism. The book is a guide to that development which parallels Rossetti's own acceptance of her self through her own life experience.

Speaking Likenesses is dedicated to Christina's mother, as so many of her works were dedicated, "in grateful remembrance of the stories with which she used to entertain her children"[7]. The book presents three stories as told by an aunt to five little girls who, like their aunt, are busy sewing while listening to the stories to pass the time. This framework of sewing relates to the "central female metaphor" used by other women poets and writers presenting the image of a "literary seamstress"[8] literally binding her story together with needle and thread. The setting of the story is the nursery of the five girls, which points to Rossetti's, as well as to other Victorian women writers', literary beginnings;

> starting out as infant poets, dramatists, or tellers of tales with enthusiastic and collaborating siblings. That not only much of the technical expertise but also some of the material of their adult work derived from the nursery circle should not surprise us.[9]

That the audience in the story is all female should not surprise us either; *Goblin Market* was also intended for the same kind of female audience. This is intended as specific discourse for women; the separation of the sexes is as much social choice as it is a cultural impediment. That the setting is the nursery points to the one place Victorian girls were allowed to express themselves; as "it was the only heterosexual world that Victorian literary spinsters were ever freely and physically to explore."[10] With the use of sewing imagery and the nursery setting, Rossetti begins to tell her tales.

Although Rossetti often uses the personal pronoun "I" in her poetry, in this story, she is more content to narrate through the speaking voice of the aunt, within the nineteenth century's predilection for masks and personae. As a spinster aunt herself, Rossetti blurs her own personal association with the tales through this device and presents a "speaking personality" which "extends itself along the filaments of the signifier... decentering the subject."[11] Rossetti, like the aunt in her story, enjoyed a close relationship with her brother William's children in her later life. By using the mask of the narrator aunt, Rossetti remains within "the romantic tradition of self-consciousness."[12] It is through this mask the stories about selfhood and personal independence will emerge.

The stories are internally framed by signifiers of maternal love: the first tale begins with a mother's morning kiss and the last one ends at night in the loving arms of a grandmother. This imagery is also indicative of women's writing in that:

> we often find... a hidden presence in the work of women writers, a buried metaphor of the mother, which shapes the style and content of the work. Just as mothers are first experienced as a presence not distinct from the self, so in literature the connection between mothers and daughters is expressed as often by the hidden maternal presence in the narrative voice as it is by explicit characters.[13]

This hidden presence of the maternal will manifest itself in a secondary frame around the stories which also defines the time periods of the stories: the first story opens in the morning, the second story takes place at tea-time, and the last story culminates in the evening. These divisions, along with the maternal presence, indicate the progressive development of the female, stretching from the morning of initial self awareness and separation from the mother to the evening of self acceptance and reunification with the maternal. This pattern is inherent in the

Persephone motif which, for the purposes of Jungian psychology, becomes the archetypal search for the female self.

The first story the aunt tells is about Flora and her eighth birthday. Instead of enjoying the party her family and friends have prepared for her, Flora pouts and complains about everything; she eventually wanders off in the garden only to descend into a hidden world of strange and malevolent children ruled by a nasty tempered birthday queen. Flora is compelled to take part in the horrible games the weird children play until she finally wakes from her nightmare and returns home to the bosom of her family. On the surface, this is a didactic tale designed to teach little girls to behave properly and not to be selfish or unreasonable. Flora and the young girls in the aunt's audience recognize that the horrible birthday queen is Flora herself: literally, her speaking likeness. Flora has been given the chance to see what she looks and sounds like to others. She learns her lesson with humility and "a conscious look in her little face that made it very sweet and winning."[14] She also learns "how to be obliging and good-humored under slight annoyances."[15] This, at least is the surface of the story.

Beneath this surface, Rossetti presents some very interesting characters in the malevolent children of Flora's fantasy. The boys, named Quills, Hooks, and Angles, inflict physical pain and humiliation upon Flora while playing games as directed by the birthday queen. At least one of these boys can be identified from Rossetti's own life; William Bell Scott, purported by Lois Mosk Packer to be Rossetti's secret lover, had been nicknamed "The Porcupine" because he "bristled with prickly quills"[16]; as an engraver by profession, Bell would have used quills as professional tools. The males are presented as human weapons, often hurting themselves as they try to hurt others in their playing. One of the games the fantasy children play is "Hunt the Pincushion" in which Flora is the designated pincushion:

> Quills with every quill erect tilted against her, and needed not a pin: but Angles whose corners almost cut her, Hooks who caught and slit her frock... all wielded longest, sharpest pins, and all by turns overtook her.[17]

The other game the children play is called "Self Help", the title of which mimics Samuel Smiles 1859 work of the same name which stresses points of personal industry and self-improvement. In Rossetti's version of Self Help, "no adventitious aids were tolerated, but each boy depended exclusively on his own resources" while the girls, in turn, are "dragged", "goffered", and "scratched" by the boys, who "did not as a body extract unmixed pleasure from Self Help."[18] Rossetti comments here on a social movement of her own time, perhaps indicating the cruelty and disregard toward others when the individual is only concerned with selfish motives.

The female children presented in this dark fantasy are named Sticky and Slime. They have no shape of their own, but take on the shape of whatever they are attached to, leaving in the wake parts of themselves as sticky or slimy substances. Set in opposition to the boys, who are made of hard, intractable surfaces, these girls are almost amorphous; they, too, partake in the games, but it is the boys who "were always the players, the girls played,"[19] as the aunt explains to her listening audience. This war between the sexes is foreshadowed in the garden when Flora's friends and siblings "tossed the apple of discord to and fro as if it had been a pretty plaything." The aunt explains that "The Apple of Discord ... is a famous apple your brothers would know all about,"[20] a witty turn on the traditional mythological symbolism of the apple of Aphrodite that figures in the *Iliad*, hence studied by the boys, but not by the girls. The remark perhaps is also indicative of Rossetti's own experience with her domineering brothers.

In presenting this story, Rossetti employs her own common poetic theme of vanity. As Flora seeks control and presence over her siblings and friends, she indulges in the vanity of pre-eminence, seeing herself as better or more worthy than the others. In her fantasy, she becomes the subject to the whims and cruelties of the monster children; the only way the spell of the fantasy is broken is when Flora tries to come to the defense of another child. The queen, in a fit of anger, hurls a huge stone at Hooks during a rock-throwing spree:

> "Oh don't, don't, don't" cried out Flora again, almost choking with sobs. But it was useless. The ponderous stone spun on ... its way to crush Hooks. Half mad with fear, Flora flung herself after it through the breach...[21].

Only through the sacrifice of her own well-being is Flora able to break the spell of the fantasy. She becomes liberated through self abnegation. Her trials have led her to this point; she has become Christ-like as the suffering servant, a motif Rossetti employs with Lizzie in the *Goblin Market*.[22] This first story operates at the basic level of intercourse between the infantile self and the world, which, for Rossetti, could often be "duplicitous, violent, and materialistic"[23]. But like Lizzie, Flora doesn't fight back, instead she finds victory and freedom by denying her egotistical self and coming to the aid of another. Aside from exemplifying the Christian ethic, Rossetti couches the lesson in a war between the sexes, demonstrating the dependency relation of women in society while offering peace (at least, personal peace) through Christian values.

The room of Flora's fantasy is lined with mirrors, echoing Rossetti's "A Royal Princess":

> All my walls are lost in mirrors, whereupon I trace
> Self to right hand, self to left hand, self in every place,
> Self-same solitary figure, self-same seeking face[24].

In this context then, all of the monster children are aspects of Flora herself. She can only exorcise the demons by denying her childlike impulses and rising to a higher plane of self-abnegation. Flora's development comes as a result of learning how to make the right choices in regards to her outward behavior toward other people. It becomes particularly feminine because much of Flora's struggles results in passive resistance to the male aggression of the monster boys. Self-abnegation, for Rossetti and many Victorians, is necessary for the individual female to move toward complete maturity.

The second story of the triad is foreshadowed in the first tale as Susan tries to control Flora's unruly party guests with a story about the frog and the tea-kettle. The aunt's nieces beg her to relate the tale, which the aunt does on the promise that the sewing would continue. The motif of Edith's descent into the forest ("to go down to the beeches"[25]) parallels that of Flora's, but this time, the companions of Edith represent the natural world. Marianne Moore once said that it is the job of the poet to present "'imaginary gardens with real toads in them'"[26]; Rossetti does exactly that with the story of little Edith.

Edith wants to light a fire for the "gypsy tea" that her "loving mother" has planned for the family that afternoon[27]. In this second story, the mother is an invisible presence only spoken of; she is never seen. The box of matches Edith carries into the woods are called "lucifers"[28] perhaps indicating that something particularly human, something other than the natural, is being brought into the idyllic grove.

Edith is accompanied by her dog, cat, and bird which parallel the animals that surround Flora on her birthday morning. The mirrors of the first story are transformed into a reflecting pool in the second tale. Above the pool, there is a cluster of tempting grapes Edith longs for, but they are "never in reach."[29] Try as she might, however, she cannot get the matches to light even though the forest animals come to her aid. The help they offer is conducive to their abilities: the squirrel offers to fan the flame with his tail, the mole rearranges the sticks of the fagot, and the two wood-pigeons offer to act as a bellows should a fire actually start. But the problem is that no one, not even Edith, can light a fire effectively. At this point, a fox appears and tries to get the grapes from the high vine, but he, too, is frustrated. Edith's nurse then comes to the rescue; she chastises Edith for disappearing without a word and exhorts her to return to the family waiting for her in the house.

The obvious symbolism of the Aesop fable about the fox and the grapes is presented as the vanity of reaching for something beyond one's grasp. Just as Flora had to learn about "patience and forbearance"[30] when dealing with others, Edith must learn about the same virtues regarding her own abilities. Part of the problem is that Edith is not properly prepared to do her job; she lacks the suitable tools and knowledge needed to complete her task. The natural world cannot effectively help her because they are powerless within the human realm. Personally, Edith "thought herself by no means such a very little girl, and at any rate as wise as her elder brother, sister, and nurse"; later, she is referred to as a "very wise girl", but that is just Edith's problem: she is not wise enough to know her own limitations[31].

Her pride has taken over, making Edith believe that she could do something beyond her abilities. Her situation becomes critical when Edith realizes that "Her relations, friends, and other natural enemies would be arriving, and would triumph over her"[32]. The sympathetic animals offer solutions that would only apply to other animals, such as the pigeons suggesting she simply fly away. Although they try to help, the animals always remain within the limits of their capabilities. This is what Edith, and Rossetti, learn from nature: self knowledge and self acceptance depend on personal awareness of one's own limitations. Whatever exists beyond our reach was never made for us; the grapes probably are sour simply because they were never meant to be our grapes. Acceptance of the limitations of the individual nature is the next step in the development of the self.

The animal imagery in this tale is reflected all through Rossetti's poetry, especially in *Sing-Song*, her collection of nursery poems. Since childhood, small animals were always considered favorite subjects for Rossetti's poetic themes. Interacting with such unusual animals as wombats or millipedes often provided thematic imagery for her poetry. The natural world initially discovered in her own childhood garden represents for Rossetti a divinely ordered existence that can act as a model for humans struggling toward a comprehension of God's plan. It can be a source of compassion as well as provide insight into the self and its place and purpose in the world.

Edith's failure, and that of Flora's as well, is that they are not self conscious about belonging to an order greater than themselves. Their choices are wrong because they fail to take into account the systems to which they belong. The young girls must be taught, through their inappropriate choices, that "none of them is truly single since each one's personality only exists in a dependency relation to someone else"[33]. Identity of the self must come through a relative position to the world, not through isolation from it. It is after presenting these two stories that Rossetti now presents the third part of *Speaking Likenesses*, the part that will successfully integrate the other two into a complete whole and present a unified process of female self development.

At the behest of her nieces, the aunt proceeds to tell a winter tale which opens with an approaching evening; Maggie and her grandmother are just closing up their shop. Dame Margaret is a "simple old woman"[34] known for her charitable acts and her Christian humility. She and Maggie sell the little vanities that children like Edith and Flora are indulged with. Maggie volunteers to deliver a package left behind by a doctor's family even though it means she will have to walk home in the cold dark. Carelessly, or unconsciously, soon after starting out, she suffers a fall that causes her to have a "marvelous adventure"[35].

The first episode is an encounter with the monster children from the first story; this time, however, they are weightless beings, capable of rolling and tumbling through the air. For just a moment, Maggie forgets her errand and agrees to play with the children. But as the children argue about what to play (the debate concerns the same games played in the first tale), Maggie becomes conscious of the purpose of her trip:

> She ceased jumping, she steadied her swinging basket on her arm,
> and spoke resolutely though sadly: "Thank you all, but I mustn't
> stop and play with you, because I promised Granny to make haste.
> Good-bye;" -- and off she started, not venturing to risk her decision
> by pausing or looking back.[36]

Maggie makes a very conscious decision to put her own selfish wants aside and to continue on her errand as she promised her grandmother. In doing so, she gains the capacity, the self awareness, to resist temptation. But her trials have just begun.

She next encounters a boy whose only facial feature is a large mouth "full of teeth and tusks" who accosts Maggie in an attempt to take away her basket.[37] Angrily, Maggie resists, resolute to continue on her way. She then passes a group of sleeping, snoring people; "merely to see them was enough to send one to sleep", but Maggie resists the temptation to rest.[38] She finally makes it to the doctor's house, but instead of being welcomed in and properly thanked, Maggie is sent away into the "dim, solitary, and comfortless" night[39]. In place of all the earlier forest encounters, she collects a wood-pigeon, a kitten, and a puppy (paralleling Flora's and Edith's pets) which she takes home to warm and feed at the hearth of her grandmother. Safely home, she is welcomed with "light and warmth"; after sharing her food with the small animals, Maggie and her grandmother "went to bed and to sleep."[40]

Maggie's story echoes the first two tales by repeating the Persephone motif of descent, conflict, and resolution. But in Maggie's tale, the difference is that Maggie remains conscious of the personal purpose of her actions. Maggie represents Rossetti's own "relentless quest for autonomy and self-sufficiency"[41] that allowed the poet to define the limits of her own life. Maggie goes on her journey at first to "get a glimpse of the Christmas tree"[42] at the doctor's house. But after her encounters in the forest, Maggie becomes intent on keeping her word to her grandmother. She is connected in a particular way to the world; Flora discounts her mother's kiss in expectation of the presents she is about to receive; Edith refers to her family as her "natural enemies"[43]. But not only does Maggie share real love with her grandmother, she also has a purpose in her life, true work that could give little girls confidence and positive self esteem; the work she does for and with her grandmother gives her a sense of rootedness and belonging in a world where pampered girls like Flora and Edith have none. All three descend into their adventures, but Maggie is the only one to return with self made whole through resolute determination to see her task to completion, not for a reward, not for false praise, but for the sake of remaining true to her self and her word.

That Maggie completes her journey alone and without the adulation she had hoped to receive at the doctor's house indicates the personal nature of integrity of the self. Only the self can be aware of the many small victories over temptation to vanity that it experiences. The reward becomes the epiphany of the self through personal satisfaction. Although Flora and Edith may succumb to the vanitas vanitatum by surrendering

> to an illusion, and an essentially intentional accommodation to life,
> [Maggie] struggles to maintain a distance from the deep,
> archetypal, even primordial freedom and makes, in turn, an
> essentially extensional accommodation to existence.[44]

By liberating herself from the expectations of, or the acceptance by, others, Maggie presents an alternative choice which allows her a purposeful existence.

The maternal presence which provides the internal frame of the stories returns again in the last tale as Maggie and her grandmother are reunited, echoing the archetypal reunion of Demeter and Persephone. This myth is central to any female search for the self; it differs from the male experience in that the female search does not culminate in the redemption or salvation of the individual, but centers itself in the reunification of female heritage for the communal. It is this reunification with the female past that allows Rossetti her own poetic voice:

> Perhaps more fundamentally, motherhood and the maternal body
> have been seen as the location of language and self, the place where
> the female subject and the female narrative "I" are produced and
> reproduced.[45]

The female triad that Rossetti creates in *Speaking Likenesses* is aunt/mother/crone which parallels the mythological and archetypal virgin/mother/crone. They provide the underlying intent of liberating the female self from the constricting formulas of identification in a male hierarchical society which insists on female identification through the dominant male figure of father, brother, or husband. Sticky and Slimy only have the capacity of definitive shape through whatever they attach themselves to while Maggie develops the ability to stand alone.

The imagery Rossetti employs with the male characters in the stories conforms to the Victorian writers' use of the grotesque[46]. Hooks, Quills, Angles, and the Mouth Boy point to the absurdity of the other, an inability to understand that which is not a part of the personal integration of the self. They represent the pain and alienation of a world and an order that the small heroes are not a part of and cannot gain personal definition from. The masculine element is not present in the book otherwise:

> Feminist studies have identified contemporary culture as thoroughly
> masculine in spheres such as norms, values, laws, and even

language. This masculine dominance raises the concern that any woman seeking knowledge of herself, to say nothing of seeking Self and wholeness, will be forced from the onset of her search to encounter that dominance head on[47].

Rossetti provides an option toward female self development outside societal constrictors. Self liberation from a society built and supported by a patriarchal hierarchy becomes a reformational challenge to that hierarchy. Thus, Rossetti weaves through *Speaking Likenesses* an alternative world of female self fulfillment beyond the reality of a patriarchal society:

Like Ariadne, Penelope, and Philomela, women have used their looms, threads, and needles both to defend themselves and to silently speak of themselves... For all these women, though, sewing both conceals and reveals a vision of a world in which such defensive sewing would not be necessary[48].

All of the images the three girls encounter are dreamlike images of what they cannot consciously see in themselves. Just before Maggie encounters the Mouth Boy, she considers the idea of delving into the basket of goodies for a few crumbs; her minor greed becomes personified into a devouring, greedy boy whose only function is to feed his head. Edith's own impotence is reflected in that of the woodland creatures unable to violate their own natures. Flora's poor manners and egocentric behavior become the monster children, and she their victim. The three girls descend, reconcile, and return to the aunt and the nieces; the integration of the self into wholeness and acceptance has been achieved.

Christina Rossetti sought to determine the course of her own life within her conventional society. Her poetry reflects that life and the choices she consciously made in order to pursue her poetry; those choices inherently eliminated other options, like governess, wife, or mother, she chose not to recognize for herself. But her awareness of the shortcomings of her social system and the limited choices available for female self expression is formulated in her writing. Within *Speaking Likenesses,* she presents a unity of experience that leads to the fulfillment of a particular female voice outside the realm of a patriarchal social system. She warns though this voice can only be matured through personal independence and integrity of the self, a common theme throughout Rossetti's work and her life:

"Exhaust this world and its resources... this done, is spiritual life survives, the soul will learn patience. Sit aloof and look down on the world; viewed from aloof and aloft the world's hollowness becomes apparent: this realized, the living soul strikes root in patience"[49].

It is through patience to the discipline of poetry and patience to her own religious devotions that Christina Rossetti secures a sovereignty of self; it is through

Speaking Likenesses that she shares her journey with those of us beginning our own.

[1]Packer, Lois Mosk. *Christina Rossetti.* (Berkeley: University of California Press, 1963.) 153.

[2]Auerbach, Nina. *Romantic Imprisonment.* (New York: Columbia University Press, 1985.) 115.

[3]Swann, Thomas Burnett. *Wonder and Whimsy: The Fantastic World of Christina Tossetti.* (Francestown: Marshall Jones and Co., 1960.) 15.

[4]Packer 305.

[5]Packer 306.

[6]Swann 64.

[7]Rossetti, Christina. *Speaking Likenesses.* (London: Macmillan and Co., 1874.)

[8]Gilbert, Sandra and Susan Gubar. *Madwoman in the Attic.* (New Haven: Yale University Press, 1984.) 638, 640.

[9]Moers, Ellen. *Literary Women:The Great Writers.* (New York: Oxford University Press, 1977.) 105.

[10]McGann, Jerome. "Christina Rossetti's Poems: A New Edition and a Revaluation." in *Victorian Studies.* (Winter 1980.) 237-54.

[11]Conner, Steven. "*Speaking Likenesses*: Language and Repetition in Christina Rossetti's *Goblin Market.*" in *Victorian Poetry.* 22 Winter 1984) 441.

[12]Christ, Carol. *The Finer Optic.* (New Haven: Yale University Press, 1975.) 19.

[13]Lidoff, Joan. "Viginia Woolf's Feminine Sentence: The Mother-Daughter World of *To the Lighthouse.*" in *Literature and Psychology.*(32(3) 1986.) 45.

[14]Rossetti, *Speaking Likenesses* 48.

[15]Rossetti, *Speaking Likenesses* 49.

[16][16]Packer 187.

[17]Rossetti, *Speaking* 32, 34.

[18]Rossetti, *Speaking* 35, 36, 37.

[19]Rossetti, *Speaking* 36.

[20]Rossetti, *Speaking* 10.

[21]Rossetti, *Speaking* 46-47.

[22]Rossetti, Christina.*The Complete Poems of Christina Rossetti.* ed. by R. N. Crump. vol. 1 (Baton Rouge: Louisiana University Press, 1979.) 11.

[23]Harrison, Anthony H. *Christina Rossetti: In Context.* (Chapel Hill: University of North Carolina Press, 1988.) 139.

[24]Rossetti, *Complete* 149.

[25]Rossetti, *Speaking* 52.

[26]Christ 57.

[27]Rossetti, *Speaking* 52.

[28]Rossetti, *Speaking* 55.

[29]Rossetti, *Speaking* 57.

[30]Rossetti, *Speaking* 28.

[31]Rossetti, *Speaking* 51,57.

[32]Rossetti, *Speaking* 60.

[33]McGann 245.

[34]Rossetti, *Speaking* 72.

[35]Rossetti, *Speaking* 76.

[36]Rossetti, *Speaking* 82.

[37]Rossetti, *Speaking* 85.

[38]Rossetti, *Speaking* 88.
[39]Rossetti, *Speaking* 91.
[40]Rossetti, *Speaking* 96.
[41]Harrison 16.
[42]Rossetti, *Speaking* 74.
[43]Rossetti, *Speaking* 60.
[44]Weathers, Winston. "Christina Rossetti:The Sisterhood of Self." in *Victorian Poetry*. 3(1965) 83.
[45]Michie, Helena. "Mother, Sister, Other: 'The Other Woman' in Feminist Theory." in *Literature and Psychology*. 32(4)(1986) 2.
[46]Christ 69-72.
[47]Lauter, Estella and Carol Schrieier Rupprecht. "Feminist Archetypal Theory: A Proposal." in *Feminist Archetypal Theory*. (Knoxville: University of Tennessee Press, 1985.) 221.
[48]Gilbert 642.
[49]Packer 372.

The Remote Air of a Legend:
Dame Edith Sitwell's Use of the Female Archetype

...sometimes I see a giant lion's paw on my window sill, and my three Visitors still
come -- Her with the one tooth...Her with the one eye... Her with the one ear,
waiting for some message from the Beyond.
These, the three Norns, still visit me. But soon, they will cease to do so.
Then all will be over, bar the shouting and the worms.

- Dame Edith Sitwell

For many poets of the modern era, the use of signs, symbols, and images to
create a unified body of poetry was an important concern. Poets such as W.B.
Yeats, Ezra Pound, and W.H. Auden utilized unified themes to present a universe
of their own creation, or the universe as they would have it created. Dame Edith
Sitwell was one such poet. Influenced by the Symbolist movement of French
poetry and surrounded by the notables of her own age, Sitwell created an intricate
network of archetypal signs and symbols within her poetry that made her one of
the most unique figures of modern poetry.

Her salon welcomed the likes of Virginia Woolf, Gertrude Stein, W.H.
Auden, Dylan Thomas, Noel Coward, Marianne Moore, D.H. Lawrence, Aldous
Huxley. Her portrait was painted or photographed by John Singer Sargent, Cecil
Beaton, Wyndham Lewis, Paul Tchelitchew. Musical settings for her poetry were
created by William Walton, Benjamin Britten, Humphrey Searle, and Michael
Head. Her gravestone was designed by Henry Moore. She was a patron as well as
critic of the arts. Herself a prolific writer, Sitwell's body of work includes
anthologies, histories, and criticisms of various writers, poets, and historical
figures. Her works have been translated into German, Spanish, Italian, and
Japanese. Never has a figure of twentieth century letters been so loved, or so
villified, by her critics, as Dame Edith Sitwell was in her generation.

Kenneth Clark called her poetry "a prophetic cry"[1]; Harold Acton
described her as a "hieractic figure in Limoges enamel"[2]. To her public she was the
embodiment of "the High Priestess of English poetry"[3]; to her critics, she was
accused of being all form without substance. She saw herself as an archetypal
figure, dressing her long, thin frame in rich embroideries, vibrant jewels, and hats
that resembled crowns and haloes that gave her "the aura of a twentieth century

myth"[4]. In an interview given late in her life, Sitwell acknowledged that "If I were to appear in the streets in a coat and skirt, people would doubt the existence of the Almighty"[5]. Cyril Connelly remarked, "When we come to compare the collected works of Dame Edith Sitwell with those of Yeats or Mr. Eliot, or Professor Auden, it will be found that hers have the purest intention of any; the honey may sometimes fail, but it is never adulterated"[6].

Edith Sitwell's use of the female archetype differs considerably from the manner in which the archetype is used by other modernist poets. Instead of the archetype representing the end of the poetic quest (as with David Jones) or as procreative powers gone bad (as with T.S. Eliot), Sitwell uses the female archetype to reflect her own search for self actualization as a woman and as a poet. I believe this moment of self actualization can be identified from Sitwell's own remarks concerning the composition of "The Shadow of Cain," her most mature work of her middle period. Her reaction to her own femaleness, to her position as poet-artist, and to her own evolution to the position of High Priestess-Prophetess of her age allows Edith Sitwell to become the embodiment of the archetypal female. Her body of poetry reflects this search through the female archetypes she employs at each stage of her career. It also suggests that, as a unified body of work, Sitwell's poetry can be interpreted as rebirth literature, the female quest for self actualization. Inherent in that quest are the encounters with shadows and archetypes which serve to aid the unification of the hero with ultimate objective of the quest: the unification of the self.

Born in 1887 to an already unhappy aristocratic couple, Edith Sitwell found herself to be an immediate disappointment to her parents. Her father was "born out of his century. His life ranged from the date of eleven hundred to the end of the life of Queen Anne"[7]. Her seventeen year old mother, forced into marriage, was "never more than a reminder of bondage"[8]. Edith herself never conformed to the Victorian ideals of beauty. As a result, she was locked daily and nightly into various orthopedic contraptions that were supposed to straighten her bones and reshape her nose. She called these contraptions her "Bastille"; her brother Osbert later recalled them as "a good deal of plain physical torture"[9]. Edith rebelled as much as she could within the restraints of Victorianism; her autobiography shows her childhood to be lonely and depressing:

> I... had strangely for so small a child -- indeed for any child -- the eyes of someone who had witnessed and foretold all the tragedy of the world. Perhaps I, at four years old, knew the incipient anguish of the poet I was to become[10].

Like Christina Rossetti, she took refuge in her family's gardens and delighted in the nature and the animals she befriended. Her governess took her on walks through cemeteries which eventually became incorporated in Sitwell's own poetic visions of the transitory nature of life and death. Trained in classical music and the arts, Sitwell found herself engrossed in the poetry of the masters, especially Alexander Pope. She was once punished severely for substituting in a school lesson a rousing rendition of Pope's "Rape of the Lock" in place of the more insipid "The Boy Stood on the Burning Deck"[11].

Throughout her childhood, Edith Sitwell was reminded over and over of her failure as a female, at least her own perceived failure, a view encouraged by her parents. Her relationship with her aristocratic mother was stormy at best, destructive at its worst. It was through her mother's line of descent that Edith could trace her family back to the Plantagenet kings; Edith herself strongly resembled Queen Elizabeth I. Her earliest poetic use of female archetypes reflect the family women she was surrounded by in her childhood. She once described her grandmother as "a fantastic, wave-like Chinoserie, a Laideronette, Princesse des Pagodes. Beaked like a harpy"[12]. In her poem, "Colonel Fantock," which is a diary of childhood experiences, she writes of her great grandmother in archetypal terms:

> My great grandmother bent to say good night,
> And the enchanted moonlight seemed transformed
> Into the silvery tinkling of an old
> And gentle music-box that played a tune
> Of Circean enchantments and far seas;
> Her voice was lulling like the splash of these[13].

Many of her early poems figure in grandmothers, aunts, cousins, and even maids as Edith tried to come to terms with her feelings of otherness from the traditional sense of femininity she was told she was supposed to have. Sitwell also describes her father as a shadow of a man unnconnected to his children, cold and distant:

> When she had given me her good night kiss
> There, in her lengthened shadow, I saw this
> Old military ghost with May-fly whiskers --
> Poor harmless creature, blown by the cold wind,
> Boasting of unseen unreal victories
> To a harsh unbelieving world unkind...
> He is not even dead, but Death's buffoon
> On a bare stage, a shrunken pantaloon[14].

This shadow in archetypal terms becomes the very social force that impedes Sitwell's own conception of herself. Unable to identify with the women in her life and incapable of living up to Victorian society's standards of beauty, Sitwell is left soulless, with no other identity than the costumes she chooses to wrap herself in.

Sitwell also found comfort with her governesses; the most beloved was Helen Rootham, a scholar and translator of the French poet Rimbaud. She introduced Edith to Symbolist poetry and the music of Debussey, Ravel, and Stravinsky, which would have an enormous effect on Sitwell's connection of music to poetry. As a young woman, Sitwell was allowed to leave her family home and establish Helen Rootham and herself in London for the beginning of an auspicious career.

Her earliest poetry deals with herself as daughter ("Colonel Fantock", "The Sleeping Beauty", *The Mother*) and her position in the spring of her life (*Bucolic Comedies:* "The Early Spring", "Aubade", "Gardener Janus Catches a Naiad", "Green Geese", "Springtime Jack", "The Man With a Green Patch"). Although these early poems carry the seeds for her later, more intensely developed imagery, these verses lack the maturity and self confidence of her subsequent work. Here, in this light and colorful world of green, is where Sitwell's quest for self actualization begins. Into this world of green, Sitwell enters as virgin; Edith is unto herself alone. And from this green world, she is almost creating for herself the aspect of the maternal that was absent from her own childhood; the archetypal quest would dictate that she begin in a state of nature:

> [Northrup] Frye's hero starts out in a green world of innocent nature, a "pastoral and Arcadian world, generally a pleasent wooded landscape, full of glades, shaded valleys, murmuring brooks, the moon, and other images closely linked with the female or maternal aspect of sexual imagery... the young woman hero accepts rather than fears her connection with nature; she is happy in a green world and feels threatened only by incursions from culture[15].

The nature of these early poems reflects the nature Sitwell took pleasure in during her unhappy childhood. Forced into society, into an increasingly mechanized society, Sitwell finds refuge in the one home in which she felt comfortable and secure; nature becomes the maternal aspect for her life. It is from this viewpoint of the preeminance of the natural that Sitwell becomes a critic of her society, indicting the false fronts contrary to nature and the hypocrisy of the social establishment. But her biting wit also extends to the conditions of poetry as an art as well:

> At the time I began to write, a change in direction, imagery and rhythms in poetry had become necessary, owing to the rhythmical flaccidity, the verbal drabness, the dead and expected patterns, of some of the poetry immediately preceeding us[16].

The poets of the Georgian school for Sitwell "'seemed obsessed by the predilection for sheep'"[17].

As social critic, this early period of writing concludes with her best social commentaries against those she and her brothers would term the "philistines"[18]; "Elegy on Dead Fashion", *Gold Coast Customs*, and one of the best British anti-war poems, "Still Falls the Rain" present a different, more intense, more serious tone set within the strong, clashing rhythms of the poetry as opposed to the light, natural rhythms of her earlier work. These poems indicate the "spiritual shrinkage of the world"[19] as well as mark Sitwell's acceptance as a poet-artist as well as critic.

The dramatic, public presentation of "Still Falls the Rain" in the summer of 1944 during an actual bombing raid on London takes on legendary proportions as it is combined Sitwell's predilection for performance with special effects provided by Hitler. Although the audience was understandably nervous, Dame Edith continued her reading "as if nothing were amiss"[20]. As she came to the last line of the poem, "Still do I love, still shed my innocent light, my Blood, for thee,"[21] a bomb exploded less than a mile away. The audience, amazed at Sitwell's seeming indifference to the danger and her penchant for the dramatic, responded with "deafening applause"[22].

As well as defining Sitwell as a social critic and a force to be reckoned with in British poetry, these poems signify her entry into the second phase of female development. With the creation of her own natural world, Sitwell was able to bring herself out of her childhood, her virgin stage, and into the middle stage of her life. Her personal vision of her own femaleness had undergone such immense destruction and ambivalence in her youth as to seriously damage her own self concept; "I have no nature and no character -- only personality and gusts of cold air in the midst of the blackest lonliness"[23]. Psychologically, Sitwell still had to reunite herself with her own internal maternal aspect. Sworn never to marry ("Artists should never marry"[24]), Sitwell needed to find that lost aspect of herself through her work; "it is a popular superstition that the poet is the child. It is not the poet but the poem: the most that the poet can do is to be a wise, experimenting parent"[25].

Her second stage of poetry is consumed by this search for self through the use of the Demeter/Persephone myth and the constant employment of harvest imagery; "the result is a network of interlocking cycles of birth, growth, fruition, decay, death, and rebirth"[26]. The myth of Demeter tells of the separation of mother and daughter through a patriarchal presence; there is violence in this separation that is never quite overcome, but finally compomised. Mother and daughter are reunited; Persephone emerges from the dark underworld to spend seasonal time with her mother. For women, this is an important myth of self actualization and identity that represents the unification of the mother of childhood and the woman the daughter has become. Even in traditional mythology, Demeter is a daughter of the gods, but never a wife. She offers to her own daughter a powerful regeneration, a chance at reunifying that which has been rent. The restoration of Persephone "represents psychologically... 'a re-membering or a putting back together of the mother-daughter body'"[27]. This chance for unity allows Sitwell to begin her own process of regeneration. These middle period poems show how she worked through that process.

Starting with "Invocation", "An Old Woman", "Eurydice", and "Heart and Mind", Edith Sitwell moves toward personal acceptance and even celebration of herself. Unlike the virginal female archetype that marked the early poems, these poems use the archetypal mother as principle speaker:

> I who was once a golden woman like those who walk
> In the dark heavens -- but am now grown old....[28]

> I, an old woman in the light of the sun,
> Wait for my Wanderer, and my upturned face
> Has all the glory of the remembering Day....[29]

> I am fecundity, harvest....[30]

> In the lateness of the season, I with golden feet
> That had walked in the fields of Death, now walk again....[31]

All of these poems concern themselves with "gestation, generation, and duration"[32] which point to the transitory aspect of life and the idea that from life comes death and from death, life is reborn:

> But I feared not that the stilled and chilling breath
> Among the dust... Love is not changed by Death,
> And nothing is lost and all in the end is harvest.[33]

Sitwell also includes the mythical characters of Osiris, Orpheus, the king, and Dionysus as the male presence in this series as "the 'green world lover' represents a natural Eros"[34] as well as the hieros gamos of the goddess. Although the love represented is antimarital, and in some ways, antisocial, it does serve to take the reconnected self back to a pattern of psychological health and completeness. Mother and daughter reunited leaves room for the male element to return in a nonthreatening manner as a presence and not just a shadow.

The mother figure Demeter or Eurydice offers a new kind of regeneration for the poet; "again and again, the poet exalts the lifegiving planet, and recalls the myth of Demeter in a fashion that suggests her self identification with the corn goddess, seen as another old woman who lives in the light of the sun"[35]. By unifying herself with this principle, the poet is able to emerge from the depths of Pluto's hell a purposeful being. Edith Sitwell emerges whole and healthy and able to extend herself into the most important and final period of her poetry writing. By this time, her technical experiments had ended, her lines of poetry had lengthened, and her ability to control these longer lines had improved considerably. She used "occasional rhymes, assonances, and half-assonances, used, outwardly and inwardly in the lines, to act as ground rhythm... with such long lines, I wrote of harvest"[36].

It is at this point that Dame Edith Sitwell comes to her moment of self actualization. In September 1945, she read an eyewitness account of the dropping of the atomic bomb on Hiroshima. The eyewitness described a "totem pole of dust [arising] to the sun as a witness against the power of mankind"[37]. From this imagery, Sitwell decided to write a poem about the destruction and what it portended for the world. Around the beginning of 1946, she had a dream in which these words appeared to her:

> There was great lightning
> In flashes coming to us over the floor:
> The Whiteness of the Bread --
> The Whiteness of the Dead --
> The Whiteness of the Claw --
> All this coming to us in flashes through the open door.[38]

In her own words, Sitwell describes the effect the dream had on her composition of the poem "The Shadow of Cain":

> I *dreamed* [Sitwell's emphasis] those lines about two months before
> I began to write the poem as a whole. The open door, in my dream,
> was the door of birth, through which we would come to Bread,
> Struggle (the Claw), and Death. As I used the symbol of the door in
> the poem, it is still the door of birth; but it is also the door through
> which we must find our own path. The three lightnings are still
> those three primal Realities. Reduced to these, in the very house of
> Birth and Death, having found our way in the desert of the Cold, I
> saw Spring returning.[39]

This is the moment of Sitwell's self actualization; it is the moment in which she most successfully comes to terms with her own existence. The imageries are the same imageries she used before: Birth, the Claw, and Death equal gestation, generation, and duration. But her own acceptance of her poetic vocation comes to her as a revelation. From this point onward, her use of female archetypes explodes with a power never before seen in her poetry. Her quest has led her to this end. She began by walking the green world of her past, then she descended into the underworld to reunite her own mother-daughter biunity, and now she emerges from those depths an accomplished and resurrected poet; "this return is often seen as part of the developmental pattern in women -- what Erich Neumann calls a reconnection to the Self (the archetype of wholeness and the regulating center of the personality)"[40].

When Sitwell goes through that door, she is entering her final stage of poetic and personal development as crone, priestess-prophetress of her age and era; it is indeed the door of rebirth, through which she sees the "violent Spring"[41]. Through this door, the poet receives the message in such an oracular fashion as to crystalize in her own mind her existence and purpose as a poet.

"The Canticle of the Rose" published two years after "The Shadow of Cain" marks Sitwell's persona as the female archetype herself:

> The Rose upon the wall
> Cries -- 'I am the voice of Fire:
> And in me grows
> The pomegranate splendor of Death, the ruby garnet almondine
> Dews: Christ's wounds in me shine!'[42]

She has become the archetype she only met in the grassy, green garden of her youth; she has become the mother of social criticism her society needed to hear; she has become the Prophetress of an age devoid of mythic material. Her essence is now Fire, creative, destructive, and purifying. And so Sitwell becomes the crone of prophecy; her words carry the impact of oracles. In this sense, she reaches the zenith of her career as poet-artist.

The tone of these poems in this last phase of Sitwell's poetry is far from elegiac. The most striking example of archetypal imagery used appears in "The Coat of Fire", "Medusa's Love Song", and "A Hymn to Venus." Two of these poems are titled with Goddess names; the third clothes the poet in an oraculer coat of fire. There is an understanding of the transitory nature of life combined with a sense of perpetuity, of life coming from death, which Dame Edith translated into her own conversion to Catholicism a few years later:

> Tell me that nothing dies
> But only after suffers change --
> And Folly may grow wise.
> So shall we be transmuted -- you who have grown chill,
>   and I
> Unto whose heart
> My love preferred a heart like a winding sheet of clay --
> Fearing my fires would burn his body away!...
>
> So Lady, you and I
> And the other wrecks of the heart, left by the Lion
> Of love, shall know all transmutations, each degree![43]

An old woman is speaking who represents this new, strong voice of the crone that Sitwell accepts for herself. The lines: "Pity me then -- a poor old woman who must wear a rag / Of Time's filth for a dress"[44] echo Yeats' "rag and bone shop of the heart" which he wrote in his advancing years. Her color imagery and the images of gems (which reflect the transmutation of light, the life-giving force) come to a brilliant culmination in this poem.

"Medusa's Love Song" also celebrates a female archetype rarely seen at this point in time in a positive presentation. But in this poem, Sitwell uses Medusa's awful powers as the yang, or the destructive aspect, of the previous poem's yin, powers of the creative aspect. Acknowledging the inevitability of the continuum of life, Sitwell's tone still remains strongly positive as her acceptance of self leads her to the acceptance of her own "Spring"[45] and the powers of her creative, destructive, and purifying fire.

In the last poem of this series, "The Coat of Fire", Sitwell presents a religious vision of herself clothed in a coat of fire. She has reached the pinnacle of her artistic career "Amid the thunders of the falling Dark"[46] of her own life. Sitwell embodies the very force of the archetype she has been chasing all of her life. Her persona stands above the world, and from that vantage point, the poet envisions both beginnings and endings:

> A Pillar of Fire is she in the empty dust,
> And will not change those fires into warmth for our hands,
> Said the beggars, lolling and rocking
> The heedless world upon a heaving shoulder.[47]

With these final words, Sitwell addresses the fate of those "beggars" who will not be saved through her poetic words; these will suffer the fate of conflagration she foretells with her poetic vision. It is the crystallizing point of her own poetic calling.

During the next few years, she would be awarded the title of Dame by the Queen. Her poetry readings and musical presentations achieved the status of state events. She was received on her tours through the United States as a figure of British royalty. Most of her poems after this point were written as gifts and dedications to close friends and colleagues. Plagued by ill health, Dame Sitwell spent most of her last years enjoying the position of privilege: "The Press is madly excited at my being 75, and is looking forward avidly to my funeral"[48]. She received visitors from the "throne"[49] her wheelchair had now become. Looking back on her career as a poet, she concluded that, "Poetry is, indeed, the deification of reality, and one of its purposes, among others, is to show that the dimensions of man are, as Sir Arthur Eddington said, 'Halfway between those of an atom and a star'"[50].

Dame Edith Sitwell's poetry indeed represents a unified vision of female self actualization. When W.B. Yeats was asked to choose a few of her poems for an anthology, he had to admit that the body of her work represented "a tapestry"[51] from which he would be hard pressed to pull at the individual threads. Her unified vision differs from those of her male counterparts in that she actualized herself and her life into the span of the archetypal female. Elizabeth Salter writes that "the true autobiography of Edith Sitwell is her *Collected Poems*"[52]. Sitwell's strong concern for an "architectonic interest in the order and design of all poetry, including her own"[53], dictates her repetitions of themes and symbols that would eventually lead her to a conclusive self definition.

It is her journey of self actualization that will allow Dame Edith Sitwell a more prestigious place in the canon of modern poetry as one of the best poets of the twentieth century. And although feminist critics haven't paid much attention to her work as yet, I believe there is much to be explored here. Through her life and her work, Edith Sitwell embodies the search for the female self in the modern world. And, like Demeter, she takes us on a journey through the fields of spring, down to the infernal regions of the unconscious, and back again in a transmutation of brilliant light and flashes of lightning. It is a journey no one should miss.

[1] Salter, Elizabeth. *Edith Sitwell.* (London: Oresko Books, 1979.) 18.
[2] Salter 50.
[3] Salter 19.
[4] Salter, Elizabeth. *Fire of the Mind.* (London: Michael Joseph, 1976.) 281.
[5] Salter, *Fire* 95.
[6] Salter, *Fire* 271.
[7] Salter, *Fire* 37.
[8] Salter, *Edith Sitwell* 5.
[9] Salter, *Fire* 42.
[10] Sitwell, Edith. *Taken Care Of: The Autobiography of Edith Sitwell.* (New York: Antheneum, 1965.) 16.
[11] Sitwell 43.
[12] Salter, *Fire* 23.
[13] Sitwell, Edith. *The Collected Poems of Edith Sitwell.* (New York: Vanguard Press, 1968.) 170.
[14] Sitwell, *Poems* 170.
[15] Pratt, Ann. "Spinning Among the Fields: Jung, Frye, Levi-Strauss and Feminist Archetypal Theory." in *Feminist Archetypal Theory.* eds. Estella Lauter and Carol Schreier Rupprecht. (Knoxville: University of Tennessee Press, 1985.) 109-10.
[16] Lehmann, Jogn. *A Nest of Tigers: The Sitwells in Their Times.* (Boston: Little, Brown, 1968.) 6.
[17] Lehmann 133.
[18] Lehmann 140.
[19] Mills Jr., Ralph J. *Edith Sitwell: A Critical Essay.* (Grand Rapids, Mi.: Eerdmans, 1966.) 23.
[20] Glendenning, Victoria. *Edith Sitwell: A Unicorn Among Lions.* (New York: Knopf, 1981.) 243.
[21] Sitwell, *Poems* 265.
[22] Glendenning 244.
[23] Salter, *Fire* 17.
[24] Salter, *Edith Sitwell* 14.
[25] Riding, Laura and Robert Graves. *A Survey of Modern Poetry.* (St. Clare Shores, Mi.: Scholarly Press, 1972.) 125.
[26] Ower, John. "Cosmic Aristocracy and Cosmic Democracy in Edith Sitwell." in *Contemporary Literature.* 12 (1). (University of Wisconsin Press, 1971.) 547.
[27] Pratt 113.
[28] Sitwell, *Poems* 251.
[29] Sitwell, *Poems* 255.
[30] Sitwell, *Poems* 259.
[31] Sitwell *Poems* 261.
[32] Sitwell *Poems* 258.

[33]Sitwell *Poems* 263.

[34]Pratt 103.

[35]Deutsh Babette. *Poetry in Our Time*. (New York: Columbia, 1956.) 225.

[36]Sitwell, *Poems* xiv-xlvi.

[37]Sitwell, *Poems* xiv-xlvi.

[38]Sitwell, *Poems* 368.

[39]Sitwell, *Poems* xlvii.

[40]Perera, Sylvia Brinton. "The Descent of Inanna: Myth and Therapy." in *Feminist Archetypal Theory*. (Knoxville: University of Tennessee Press, 1985.) 139.

[41]Sitwell, *Poems* 368.

[42]Sitwell, *Poems* 373.

[43]Sitwell, *Poems* 344-45.

[44]Sitwell, *Poems* 343.

[45]Sitwell, *Poems* 341.

[46]Sitwell, *Poems* 361.

[47]Sitwell, *Poems* 363.

[48]Sitwell, *Taken Care Of* 246.

[49]Salter, *Fire* 292.

[50]Sitwell, *Poems* 423.

[51]Mills 18.

[52]Salter, *Fire* 293.

[53]Brophy, James. *Edith Sitwell: The Symbolist Order*. (Carbondale: Southern Illinois University, 1968.) xv.

Hieros Gamos and the Androgynous Mind:
Serving Eternity for Supper in Virginia Woolf's *To The Lighthouse*

All this pitting of sex against sex, of quality against quality, all this claiming of superiority and imputing inferiority, belong to the private school stage of human existence where there are "sides," and it is necessary for one side to beat another side...

- Virginia Woolf

The concept of marriage for Virginia Woolf becomes more actualized as the marriage of the female and male aspects of the individual mind. She works this concept into and throughout her novel *To the Lighthouse* by portraying the inherent sterility of traditional male and female roles in the characterizations of the purely, and culturally defined, male figures and the purely, and culturally defined, female figures. Woolf criticizes these roles as constricting and limiting for the creative human mind: "It is fatal to be a man or woman pure and simple; one must be woman-manly or man-womanly"[1]. In *A Room of One's Own*, she offers her own solution for the alternative: the androgynous mind. This would open the way for a new kind of thinking and new ways of conceptualizing reality as well as creativity.

As Woolf sees two people, a man and a woman, enter a taxi together, she conceptualizes the "collaboration [which] has to take place between the woman and the man before the act of creation can be accomplished. Some marriage of opposites has to be consummated"[2]. This marriage of opposites does take place in her novel *To the Lighthouse*, but it doesn't concern itself with Mr. and Mrs. Ramsay, or their children, or even the matrimonial match Mrs. Ramsay seeks for the artist Lily. Instead, this marriage of opposites concerns itself with the Ramsay house and the nature that surrounds it in the second section of the book entitled "Time Passes." Here, the two opposites, the man-made construction of the house, and nature, always a female archetype, combine to create something never before conceived of: the house and nature combine to form a structure that is neither a house nor nature in their truest forms. Within "Time Passes" lies the purpose of the theory that motivates the novel. Here, the purely male patriarchal construct of the house and the purely female nature combine to form a new reality, a new construct of androgyny. Even though this new construct is destroyed when Mr. Ramsay again imposes his male, and cultural, sense of order upon the house, this sense of androgyny survives in the children Cam and James.

Woolf's criticism of the traditional marriage between the "angel of the house" and the patriarchal figurehead is obvious, but what is less obvious is this development of the androgynous mind, which Lily, James, and Cam come to realize by the end of the novel. Any other character so completely retained in either the purely female or the purely male thought processes and cultural constructs is either destroyed or left sterile. That makes "Time Passes" as well as the symbol of the lighthouse the telescopic center of the novel's theme. Throughout the novel, Woolf describes marriage and its various outcomes: Mr. and Mrs. Ramsay share a long standing, long suffering marriage until Mrs. Ramsay's death; Mr. Banks is a widower; Mr. Carmichael has been thrown out by his wife; Mr. Tansley ultimately marries but he is painted in such unmatrimonial terms that one shudders to think of his unimaginative married state. No wonder Lily Briscoe decides to remain single.

In using the modernist techniques of organization, Woolf concentrates on the significant moments in her characters' lives to give a post-impressionist, almost cubist, presentation of the inter-subjective perspective to emphasize the importance of the moment that expands in space what is significant in time. Lily, the artist, is constantly shifting her perspective in relation to her paintings; this is why she survives. She makes the transition from looking (as perspective) to vision (as insight). There is also a sense of the Demeter/Persephone myth, but with a twist. Lily, whose name denotes her virgin stage, seeks unity with the archetypal mother figure of Mrs. Ramsay, but it is the mother who descends to the netherworld while the daughter waits for her return. Once Lily gives up the idea of unity with Mrs. Ramsay, she is then able to complete her painting. She is seeking definition, but discovers that definition of self must take place within the individual because all attempts of completion of self through traditional marriage are ultimately sterile. Even the fact that Mrs. and Mr. Ramsay are referred to only by the names that denote their marriage, and not their individual persons, infers that neither is female nor male at this point, but instead one product of cultural marriage. Neither has a subjective existence without the other, no power in relationships outside of their own. They can only conceive of themselves in the dependencies of others upon them. Such binary oppositions of masculine and feminine rigidly structure men and women and promise only the complete collapse of communication.

The effect of writing with the modernist emphasis on the moment allows the characters a free play of consciousness like the same free play of creation seen in the section "Time Passes." Order is not determined by chronology or history (although both take their tolls on the characters), but by the play of separate consciousness's transcending time and history. Order then becomes the creation of the artist, be that artist a painter, a writer, or any individual seeking meaning through subjective order. Permanence is linked with death while plurality and multiplicity of perspectives are linked with life and imagination.

We watch the figures move about in and outside of the house through the windows Woolf provides. But because we are viewing this family through Woolf's frame of narration, we see only that which appears in our frame of reference as readers. Like Lily, we see into and out of these windows, but our vision is limited by what the window itself frames. In the same way, we see only what Woolf wants us to see through her choices of what to include and what to edit. The window frame for Woolf as author is the book itself framed by margins of space. An even more interior referent is Woolf's use of a particular character's perspective in relation to the other characters and events within the Ramsay home. The first section of the novel, "The Window," allows us (like some of the characters in the novel) to become voyeurs in these lives. And just as Woolf provides her own perspective to describe the family, we use our own perspectives to define what her words mean to us. Reality becomes multi-dimensional instead of the thoroughly defined, flat plane of existence that the stodgy and traditional Mr. Ramsay would like us to believe.

> Clearly the mind is always altering its focus, and bringing the world
> into different perspectives... But there may be some state of mind in
> which one could continue without effort because nothing is
> required to be held back...after being divided, it had come together
> again in a natural fusion. The obvious reason would be that it is
> natural for the sexes to cooperate...The normal and comfortable
> state of being is that when the two live in harmony together,
> spiritually co-operating...Coleridge perhaps meant this when he said
> that a great mind is androgynous[3].

Woolf could be describing the "Time Passes" section of the novel as well as those two people entering and sharing the taxi together. Through time and the elements of nature, the Ramsay house, once a home for inside things to go out and outside things to come in, melds with its environment. Creation takes place and produces something that is neither male nor female, house nor nature. Left in a free play of existence unfettered by cultural prescriptives or calendar pages, this marriage produces something new: the androgynous.

In archetypal terms, the trinity of the virgin, mother, crone can be interpreted as Cam, Lily, and Mrs. Ramsay. Cam is still just a girl as the novel opens, free-spirited, beyond social compunctions; Cam exalts in her free play with nature. Lily is an artist, and as such, a mother to the creative process. Through her art, Lily longs for the right combination of color, shape, and composition that will allow her creation meaning in a social context. Mrs. Ramsay is the crone of the threesome, divining the connections between people, time, and mutability. The idea of her serving "eternity" as an entree is simply delicious. As Mrs. Ramsay is dishing out a particularly "tender piece" she feels that "there is a coherence in things, a stability; something, she meant, is immune from change, and shines out"[4], it is this aspect of Mrs. Ramsay seeing beyond the obvious and the mundane that marks her as the crone.

In another sense, the three sectioned structure of the novel can also be interpreted as the stages of virgin, mother, crone. The first section, "The Window", represents the virginal self absorption of youth, only seeing through the frame of the window which limits one's view depending on where the individual (or the author) is standing. The second section, "Time Passes", defines the birthing of something new and as yet undefined. This part of the novel deals with the creation of a new invention, a new structure: the intercourse of house and nature, male and female, who give birth to the androgynous. The third section, "The Lighthouse", is the fruition of legacy, history, and death of the old order. Cam and James are the virgins who have reconnected with their past, not for its repetition, but for the purpose of applying their new knowledge to the future, ensuring human survival. Lily's representation of Mrs. Ramsay as a purple triangle denotes the blending of red (female) and blue (male) into purple (androgyny); the triangular shape denoting the trinity of woman's existence: virgin, mother, and crone.

The lighthouse itself represents the perfect merger of male (the tower) and female (the light/life source). Just as the lighthouse draws ships and boats to safe harbor, Mr. and Mrs. Ramsay draw to their house the walking wounded of traditional marriage and gender constructs. The Ramsays' guests seek some kind of salvation through their relationships with their hosts. But even the old salt Macalister, toward the end of the novel, comments about the shipwrecks that occur even with the safe guidance of the lighthouse by reciting, "'We perished...each alone'"[5], indicating that no matter what connections do we make, no matter what beacon of light we follow, ultimately, it is the human condition to die alone.

The new creativity that Woolf endorses includes the acceptance and the integration of the female and male principles inherent in every human mind. By bringing these disparate elements together, Woolf hopes for a new realization, and perhaps even new definitions, for what it is to be a woman or a man, especially in a social construct. In an era of symbolic literary fragmentation, Woolf prefers to see that the fragments we perceive have more to do with the passage of time than the state of the world. By fragmenting the moment, Woolf demonstrates that the perception of time is also a human construct and as changeable and malleable as the constructs of social genders. She also understands that woman's reality is dependent upon her perceiving all moments of time, whether great or small, as the meaningful summation of one's life. Mrs. Ramsay ascends to the crone's position of the hero's cycle by being able to connect those moments of time into a grander vision of the inter relatedness of all life, and she returns this wisdom to her dining community in the form of serving eternity for supper. And just as her children see their trips to the lighthouse as mystical, exotic events, Woolf hopes that one day we can all make the trip, not for science, not for adventure, but as a matter of pure joy.

[1]Woolf, Virginia. *A Room Of One's Own*. New York: Harcourt Brace Jovanovich, 1989. 104
[2]Woolf 104.
[3]Woolf 97-98.
[4]Woolf, Virginia. *To the Lighthouse* (New York: Harcourt Brace Jovanovich, 1955) 158.
[5]Woolf 247.

The Circuitry of Women's Lives:
Zora Neale Hurston's Journey of Self Actualization

I love myself when I am laughing... and then again when I am looking mean and impressive.

                                                    - Zora Neale Hurston

When Zora Neale Hurston's novel of female development, *Their Eyes Were Watching God*, first appeared, it was unusual for several reasons. First, Hurston constructed a female hero, Janie, who would travel through her life on her own quest for self actualization. But instead of leaving her predominantly black community, Janie instead quests within the black community for the meaning and purpose of her life. She begins this quest in a fashion remarkably similar to the Sumerian goddess Inanna, who opens her own quest while sitting under an apple tree, rejoicing at her own vulva. Janie too begins her story under a pear tree in West Florida:

> Janie saw her life like a great tree in leaf with the things suffered, things enjoyed, things done and undone. Dawn and doom was in the branches....[1]
> It was a spring afternoon in West Florida. Janie had spent most of the day under a blossoming pear tree in the backyard. She had been spending every minute that she could steal from her chores under that tree for the last three days[2].

Words like "snowy virginity of bloom", "rose of the world", "quested", "gold", "bee", "thousand sister-calyxes"[3], "garden", "Oh, to be a pear tree -- *any* tree in bloom!", "With kissing bees singing the beginning of the world!"[4], Hurston begins the rich association of female archetypes that places Janie into her own burgeoning body and the beginning of her life. She is waiting for something to happen to her; she is waiting for a lover who would be her partner in her "struggle for life"[5]. Her grandmother, her sage-femme, sets Janie up in a loveless marriage that only stifles and threatens to suffocate Janie; but her grandmother explains her motivations by saying, "'T'ain't Logan Killicks Ah wants you to have, baby, it's protection'"[6]. But that protection proves to be illusory, so Janie eventually leaves him for another man.

The tree associations continue as her grandmother explains the plight of black people by saying, "'You know, honey, us colored folks is branches without roots and that makes things come around in queer ways'"[7]. Janie sets off from her first husband because she is searching for some larger community to belong: "She had been getting ready for her great journey to the horizons in search of *people* [Hurston's emphasis]; it was important to all the world that she should find them and they find her"[8]. As her grandmother tells Janie the story of her own life, she imparts to Janie her heritage as well as her grandmother's dream for Janie: "'Ah wanted you to look upon yo'self'"[9]; Janie must first come to terms with her self before she can adequately come to terms with the people around her. She will not find what she is seeking in the outside world. Her grandmother understands that Janie's development and maturity depend on how well Janie accepts her own voice as authority enough in her life. Janie, of course, as indicative of the virgin stage of female development seeks verification of self in the world around her. During Janie's second marriage to Jody, the mayor of an all black town, Hurston uses the word white several times, denoting Janie's virgin aspect at the beginning of her life cycle. Despite the fact that this is Janie's second marriage, Hurston implies that her hero is still within the virgin aspect of her life cycle; only true love, a *hieros gamos*, will empower Janie to go beyond the virgin aspect to her more social phase of motherhood.

While married to Jody, she does discover speech as a form of power, a power so strong that Jody tries to limit her uses of speech so as not to show up her own man:

> Time came when she fought back with her tongue as best she could, but it didn't do her any good. It just made Joe [Jody] do more. He wanted her submission and he'd keep on fighting until he felt he had it[10].

Hurston uses the words "Virgin Mary", "daisy field", and "she wasn't petal-open anymore"[11] to indicate Janie's stuck position in the virgin phase of development. It becomes clear to Janie that Jody will not allow her any more personal growth for herself, even though she knows she has discovered her own voice. Instead, Janie turns her attentions from Jody to "some man she had never seen. She had an inside and an outside now and suddenly she knew how not to mix them"[12]. The stronger Janie gets, the weaker Jody becomes until his death becomes imminent. Although Jody can't forgive Janie's lack of feeling for him, Janie refuses to be saddled with his guilt: "'Tain't dat, Jody. Ah ain't here tuh blame nobody. Ah'm just tryin' tuh make you know what kinda person Ah is befo' it's too late'"[13]. And despite her defiance, when Janie looks at herself in the mirror for the first time in a long time, she sees that "the young girl was gone, but a handsome woman had taken her place"[14]. It is after Janie's moment of self awareness that Tea Cake enters her life. Together, they are a balanced pair; unlike Jody, Tea Cake appreciates the kind of woman Janie has become. Tea Cake's real name is Vergible Woods, another archetypal reference to the sacred groves of the goddess, as well as a referent back to Janie's own wish of being a tree. She knows she can grow in the woods that Tea Cake will provide her. When her community criticizes Janie's next choice for a husband, she refuses to bend to their opinions because, as she puts it, "'Ah wants tuh utilize mahself all over'"[15]. She is strong enough now to incorporate her grandmother's old advice about seeking her authentic self with the creation of new ways of living: "'Ah done lived Grandma's way, now Ah mean tuh live mine'"[16]. But like Psyche and Eros, Janie and Tea Cake must work out their relationship through the issue of trust. Once settled in a farm community (continuing that connection of woman/nature, soil/soul), black music and singing enter their lives through Tea Cake's talent with the guitar that hangs around his neck by a red cord.

Each time Janie travels, she descends deeper and deeper into Florida until she finally arrives at the Everglades with her third husband, and only lover, Tea Cakes. With him, Janie now enters her mother aspect. Although she does not give birth to any children, their house becomes the center of their small black community, with Tea Cakes and Janie feeding and caring for those around them: "Tea Cake's house was a magnet, the unauthorized center of the 'job'"[17]. The fertility of the black soil mirrors the fertility of Janie's mother aspect. She and Tea Cake are surrounded by the lush growth of the fields, and the wildness of their neighbors' dancing and singing; "The house was full of people every night"[18]. The images and names of food, its cooking, its growing, its flavors and its smells, connect Janie's house to the nurturance of the community that is so prevalent in the socially oriented mother stage.

Janie has also learned how to read the natural signs of the coming hurricane, even though Tea Cake refuses to take those signs seriously. The force of the storm is considered to be a deity itself: "They seemed to be staring at the dark, but their eyes were watching God"[19]. It is interesting to note that the sheer force of nature (always a female archetype) is equated with God's actions In what becomes an apocalypse of archetypal signs, Janie finds herself and her lover trying to survive the raging lake that has taken over the land. To save herself, Janie grabs hold of the tail of a swimming cow that has a "massive built dog"[20] sitting on her back. When this hell-hound threatens Janie, Tea Cake plunges after her and drowns the dog, but not before the dog bites his cheek, symbolic of the mythic kiss of death. Tea Cake then develops rabies from the bite, and Janie unwillingly enters her last and final stage of female self actualization: that of crone, harbinger of death and eternity. And "Tea Cake, son of Evening Sun, had to die for loving her"[21] which becomes for Janie the "the meanest moment of eternity"[22]. When Tea Cake threatens Janie while in a rabid state himself, Janie draws her rifle and shoots him dead. Her silence at her subsequent trial for his murder signifies the inner peace that Janie has now discovered as crone; "She just sat there and told and when she was through she hushed"[23]. Her power of speech, ignored as a maiden, found while married to Jody and developed with Tea Cake, can be withheld as well as expressed; she deliberately controls her power of narration now as the crone of death as well as life. This is her story to tell or not to tell. She knows that what she did, she had to do; there was no sense in trying to explain her actions to the white folks in court. She has already passed sentence on herself.

After being released by the court, Janie prepares a spectacular funeral for her beloved Tea Cake, who goes to his grave "like a Pharaoh to his tomb"[24]. Like Osiris and Dumuzi before him, his death as well as his life is celebrated as one of nature's necessary sacrifices. Janie then returns to her all-black community, bringing with her seeds to plant in remembrance of Tea Cake and her stories and lessons learned while in her descent in the Everglades. As crone, Janie returns in order to reconnect to the young and less experienced. She is now the sage-femme who will guide the young on their searches for their authentic selves. And whoever might be brave enough to actively accept the role of hero will be rewarded with the peace and wisdom and serenity that Janie now commands. She is one with the universe around her, realizing that in her old community "was peace. She pulled in her horizon like a great fish-net. Pulled it from the waist of the world and draped it over her shoulder. So much of life in its meshes! She called in her soul to come and see"[25]. According to the hero cycle, Janie returns as crone to pass on to her society the teachings of one who has achieved a worthy education. Hurston ends the book with Janie ready to impart her wisdom to her friends, which connects beautifully back to the opening of the book wherein Janie begins her story, indicating the eternal circuitry of women's lives and the hero cycle, thereby making true the words of another black bildungsroman novelist: "the end is in the beginning, and lies far ahead"[26].

The Eros (Cupid) and Psyche story echoes all through Janie and Tea Cake's relationship. The myth represents the female experience with the *hieros gamos*, the sacred marriage. Many male novelists use the consummation of the *hieros gamos* to end the stories about female (and sometimes even male) characters. But women, and women writers, understand that the *hieros gamos* is only one event in a life's span. The *hieros gamos* -- like giving birth -- changes a woman by adding definition to a part of her life's experiences. Even cultural myths demonstrate that a woman's life continues past (or in spite of) the *hieros gamos*. There are always adventures after the marriage which tend to indicate that human development is more than just reproduction.

In the Eros and Psyche myth, Eros comes to Psyche nightly for lovemaking with the proviso that Psyche should not try to look upon him. But Psyche's curiosity overwhelms her, and she attempts to steal a glance of her lover while he sleeps. When a drop or two of oil from her lamp splashes on him, Eros awakens and in anger flies away. Her "sin" can be mitigated, however, when Aphrodite, mother to Eros, challenges Psyche to perform tasks that would redeem her in her future mother's-in-law eyes. Psyche completes all the tasks set before her, sometimes with the help of animals or nature who pity poor Psyche. The last task is to steal Persephone's beauty box, so that Aphrodite may know the secret of true beauty. In a passage that represents a re birthing of Psyche, she descends to the underworld and eventually gets the box. On her return to the natural world, Psyche chooses to disregard Aphrodite's order of not looking into the box. Upon opening it, she finds the box empty. Aphrodite forgives Psyche, and she and Eros then marry with the goddess's approval. But the story does not end on the marriage note; instead, a child is born from Psyche and Eros, indicating that the purpose of the *hieros gamos* is the continuation of the human species.

Psyche's opening of the beauty box marks her acceptance of self assertion. All her trials teach her that no one will place constraints upon her again. Also, Psyche finds that it is the active acceptance of self and the knowledge of the female legacy that constitutes true beauty. The search Psyche takes on is the search for the acceptance of self. What she discovers in that box -- knowledge -- places Psyche in the same company of Eve and Pandora. The fact that Psyche must search for a box -- an obvious symbol for the womb -- denotes the descent into self that virgins (re: women unto themselves) make in searching for self definition and actualization.

Janie, too, takes that same descent into self and discovers her strengths within her relationship with Tea Cake. There is an immeasurable distance between a woman defining her self through a man, and a woman who defines her self through the experience of a relationship with a man. The *hieros gamos* doesn't have to be a positive one, either. In *Barren Ground*, Dorinda is motivated to succeed despite her tragic love affair with the dissipated Jason. It is after her trials that she finds she really didn't want Jason after all. In *Jane Eyre*, Jane returns to Rochester only after she proves herself to be self-reliant. She comes back an equal match for Rochester. Now, she can marry him.

Janie, too, retains her sense of self within her marriage to Tea Cake. This powerful marriage of equals becomes the center of their community, for nurturing, for strength, and for celebrations of life and death. The myths about marriages of equals insures the survival of the human species: Isis and Osiris, Inanna and Dumuzi, Adam and Eve, and even Janie and Tea Cake.

Zora Neale Hurston has enriched the study of African-American women and African-American culture through her writings and her anthropological records about her own heritage. Well in touch with the folklore and the songs and rituals of the black South, Hurston refused to define her culture as simplistic or primitive, or by using the words and language of white America. In *Their Eyes Were Watching God*, she not only tells the story of Janie, she also records the nuances of a kind of woman's culture that could celebrate their life stages at every step of the way on their own journeys.

---

[1]Hurston, Zora Neale. *Their Eyes Were Watching God*. New York: Harper & Row, 1990. 8.
[2]Hurston 10.
[3]Hurston 10.
[4]Hurston 11.
[5]Hurston 11.
[6]Hurston 14.
[7]Hurston 15.
[8]Hurston 85.
[9]Hurston 19.
[10]Hurston 67.
[11]Hurston 67.
[12]Hurston 68.
[13]Hurston 81.
[14]Hurston 83.
[15]Hurston 107.
[16]Hurston 108.
[17]Hurston 126.
[18]Hurston 127.
[19]Hurston 151.
[20]Hurston 157.
[21]Hurston 169.
[22]Hurston 175.
[23]Hurston 178.
[24]Hurston 180.
[25]Hurston 184.
[26]Ellison, Ralph. *Invisible Man* (New York: Quality Paperback Book Club, 1994) 5.

Epilogue: To Argue The Archetypal Past

Look into the night skies. If you can locate Orion as he crosses over from the southeast to the southwest, you can watch one of the oldest dramas taking place: one that has been watched by generations of humans who have played giant games of connect-the-dots with the stars. Near to Orion's outstretched arm and slightly higher up in the sky, the horns of the constellation Taurus remain just outside of the reach of this mighty hunter. These stars, and others, form the basis for the star religion of the ancient Egyptians, more ancient than the pyramids built thousands of years after the star religion had taken an eternal hold on the Egyptian imagination. In *The Orion Mystery*, the authors make a highly credible case for the architecture of the pyramids at Giza to be based on the assembly of stars in the night skies, so clearly visible to these ancient people. The Giza pyramids, the authors contend, mimic the stars in the belt of Orion (Osiris to the Egyptians), while the other pyramid placements imitate the head of Taurus (Osiris' brother Set) and Isis (Sirius).

Osiris begins his run across the sky around mid-April; his appearance marked for Egyptians the continuation of the Isis-Osiris myth which explained the annual flooding of the Nile and the beginning of the fertile growing time along its banks with the annual death and resurrection myth of Osiris and his sister/lover Isis. Born from their mother Nut the sky and their father Geb the earth, Isis and Osiris become lovers. Set, brother to Nut, becomes jealous of his nephew, and Osiris is killed. Some variations of this myth recount how his body is cut into fourteen pieces, and then these pieces are buried all around the Nile basin. Isis, distraught over the loss of her beloved, searches for the pieces of his body which she then re-members. Unable to find his penis, however, Isis constructs a wooden one; after resurrecting her lover, they make love, and Isis conceives. She gives birth to her son Horus, destined to rule in the old king's place. The story is as old as humans are: the old king must die every year so that the young king can take his place and fertility be insured. It is a vegetative myth that demonstrates early human abilities to draw conclusions about life and death from the vegetation that surrounded them. Winter had to end so that spring could return. And the goddess in all of these myths is as constant as the earth beneath these believers' feet. Spring impregnated the earth with the creation of new life. That same life was destined to die every winter, and hopefully, grow back in the spring either perennially or by new seed being planted into the ground. In these myths, death is just as necessary as life is. If the old did not die, if the winter refused to come, then spring would be impossible. The Isis/Osiris myth is only one version of the same story told for generations and venerated as religion in cultures all around the world.

Robert Bauvel and Adrian Gilbert make quite a credible argument for the deliberate construction of the pyramids on earth as a mirror to the celestial skies above. The annual drama that played itself out among the stars was constructed now in literal concrete form on earth. The purpose of the duplication of the stars' placements on earth was to send the spirits or the souls of the dead to the after-life where they would be reborn into the celestial realm of Isis and Osiris. In this same way, some of the huge, prehistoric animal ground etchings may be better understood when viewed with a people's or a tribe's interpretations about the stories that their stars and their skies tell.

In the Egyptians' skies, they saw Osiris (Orion) rise and follow after his brother Set, denoted by the triangle formation of three stars. But what if we take those three stars as a symbol for a much older, more holy and sacred object of ancient humans: the triangular uterus. Many scholars, both academic and feminist, have determined the importance and the primacy of the triangle as symbolic of the center of the female's ability to procreate. Marija Gimbutas, Barbara G. Walker, and Judy Grahn are three such scholars who have interpreted pre-literate markings and rituals for ancient peoples. And, in that same regard, instead of seeing a "belt" on Orion, why can't we see that belt as a more primal symbol: man's erect penis. Now if we look to the night sky to see what many ancient people saw, we have the constant and forever chase through the night of man and woman. And man constantly pursuing woman: the oldest story in anyone's book. Remember the scientific symbols used to denote male and female even to this day: the female sign is illustrated by a circle with a small cross attached to it at the bottom, the cross with three points remaining open indicating the uterus; the male symbol is a circle with a small arrow attached at an upward angle as an erect penis. This leads us to stretch into one more direction. If Orion's belt was originally supposed to be man's penis, why was it eventually interpreted as clothing? Is there a connection, however cosmic or irrational for academic standards, of Adam and Eve leaving Eden with their fig leafs attached after the discovery of their nakedness and their transgression with the apple? Did Orion's penis become his "belt" when the same modicum of modesty ensued? Was viewing the triangular uterus as a bull's head more comfortable to growingly patristic societies? The bull's (or cow's) head was more symbolic of a woman's sexual organs: ovaries attached to Fallopian tubes and both attached to the uterus. This same configuration looks remarkably like the head of a cow or bull:

> The identity of the bull with uterus and regenerative waters
> accounts for its role as the principal sacrificed animal in the drama
> of creation... Its central position [in Paleolothic art] probably

derives from the intimate relationship between the bison and the Goddess; the fact that the woman and the bison both have a pregnancy of nine months may help to account for this connection... This similarity... is likely to have been discovered with the development of the excarnation process of burial... it can be seen how the female uterus and the fallopian tubes form a simulacrum of the head and horns of the bull... when the body is laid flat, they [the fallopian tubes] would be turned upwards, as they would have been observed during the excarnation process. If we note that some representations of the bull's head in Neolithic art show the horns capped with rosettes or stars, then the similarity is much greater... The Egyptian hieroglyph for uterus depicts the two-horned uterus of the cow.[1]

This predominant Egyptian myth of Isis and Osiris does correspond to the second stage of Joseph Campbell's four stage development of mythology. This stage marks the recognition of paternity in that the female deity and the male deity create together. The first stage of the female deity creating from her own body is still reflected in the Egyptians' notion of Nut as the sky goddess. But Geb has now joined her in the act of creation; they become the same yin and yang of other creative couples: Inanna and Dumuzi, Adam and Eve, Isis and Osiris. And although the development of the third stage (male deity creating life from the destruction of the female body, i.e. Marduk and Tiamat) and the fourth stage of mythology (male deity creating *ex nihilo*, out of nothing) indicates the sublimation and even the negation of the female principle in the developing patriarchy; the night skies have never lied. The female and the male principles of creation chase each other eternally in a game that does not end.

Is it so preposterous to connect this mythology to Virginia Woolf's notion of the androgynous mind? In her ground breaking essay, *A Room of Her Own*, Woolf suggests that the acceptance of the female and male principles of the individual mind should be developed equally, which would then, in turn, create a whole new mind-set: a sort of yin/yang universe within us all. And because that creative mind would be judged as neither female nor male, a new kind of thinking could then follow. And a new kind of creativity could then be born from this androgynous mind. The second section of her book *To the Lighthouse* records the merging of the neglected Ramsay house after the mother's death with the nature that surrounds it. The house, a man-made structure symbolizing the male principle, is opened by the winds, the branches of trees, and small creatures of nature, all representative of the female principle, allowing nature to move inside the house. Both merge to form a different structure which is neither house nor nature. The structure itself becomes androgynous, a new creation never conceived before. Of course, the house is eventually cleaned out and restored, but it is still the nature around the house that provides the final influences for the growth of Cam and James, Mrs. Ramsay's youngest children. These children survive and thrive by combining the best of both their parents. Unlike their all-male brother Andrew, who is killed in war, or their all-female sister Prudence, who dies in childbirth, Cam and James have horizons opened up to them in their acceptance of what is both male and female within them. The house, in the second section of the book, becomes symbolic of the androgynous mind structure Woolf calls for in *A Room of One's Own*. Woolf says that the recognition of both the male and female within all of us is necessary to our survival. So says the night skies.

And Janie would agree from Zora Neale Hurston's *Their Eyes Were Watching God*. She finds her celestial balance with her lover Tea Cake. It is through their sharing, or valuing each other's unique perspectives, that their love fills the universe even after Tea Cake's death. Their love story will become part of the mythology of their community. The story about that star drawn man following that star drawn woman is told in culture after culture, century after century, as the source and the only real meaning that humans can ascribe to life. The divine spark in each of us can be seen in the stories that the stars tell.

We often think about the effects on modern culture because of the media we chose to value the most: television. But consider its ancient ancestor: the night skies, faithfully repeated season after season. Talk about reruns: we've been watching reruns for as long as we were able to define the skies as a reflection, Judy Grahn might call it a metaform, of our own earthly conditions. And as we are split into sexes, we make our interpretations of those stories and their meanings according to female experience or according to male experience. But to define an androgynous experience, being neither male nor female, would allow the valuing of both as necessary to the survival, the propagation, and the celebration of the human species.

And since we have had more than enough time spent on the male hero's assumption of his divinity in procreation, it is of primary importance to recognize and value the female hero in those stories. The sacred marriage, the children born never stop the mythic female hero from her own heroic destiny: the search and acceptance of self. We need to recognize and validate a mega-myth for the development of women as heroes of their own journeys of self actualization. Not so much for their connections to social life, but as moral beings who can and do hold up fifty percent of the skies. Maybe that is enough reason as to why we should covet stage two in the development of mythology. Maybe that perfect balance of female and male was our Eden, our Paradise lost, our Nirvana or Great Spirit. Maybe that is precisely why we should seek that balance today.

Even Jane in *Jane Eyre* leaves her beloved Rochester to continue her search for her own origins and her own legacy. When she has discovered her true family and her past, she hears Rochester calling for her. His three cries, the image of the crossroads and the crows, and Jane's own statement, "'I am my own mistress'"[2] indicates her growth and development as crone in that she finally defines herself, instead of allowing Rochester, or anyone else, to define her.

Most zoologists would agree that the primary function of all life is the survival and reproduction of the species. This would lead us to believe that the primary activity beyond sustenance must be sex. But we hesitate to define humans as mere sexual animals. Our so-called higher brain functions would not allow ourselves to identify with what we think of as subordinate life forms. But we are mammals who have survived this long by sustaining and reproducing ourselves through the ages. And as mammals, we have innate behavioral instincts to seek food and desirable sex partners who would insure the transmission of genetic materials to the next generation. When a healthy, human baby is born, it will begin to suck almost immediately; its instinct is to feed itself by nursing from its mother's breasts. A newborn human infant still retains patterns of behavior that can insure its survival. If startled, a newborn will quickly extend its arms and legs out from its body; behavioral scientists believe this to be an ancient instinct that allows newborns to save themselves from falling out of trees by grabbing nearby branches. Newborn infants also have a swimming instinct; if placed in water over their heads, they will kick their legs frog-like and paw the water with their hands. They will also instinctually hold their breaths and open their eyes. Instincts like these serve to indicate how closely we resemble our cousin mammals. If we resemble them here, is it not reasonable to infer that we might be like them in other basic ways, like sex?

Many different mammals demonstrate mating behaviors that include the show of fancy or bright colors, mating calls, scents, and tactile sensations. The males usually show aggression toward other males who might encroach upon their prospective mates or families. Many animals participate in head-butting contests, like the buffalo and the long horned sheep, whose basic equipment includes thick skulls or massive fur patches or horns used to intimidate rivals. The more successful male guarantees the transmission of his genes to another generation. This kind of instinctual behavior can be seen in human male aggression as well. For whatever the sociological or anthropological reasons involved, male humans are responsible for, and actively involved in, the constant warfare that spans our existence. Male aggression in mammals is primarily caused by the sexual rivalry of two males for a female mate. It has often been said that men go to war because the women are watching. Many professional sports teams still retain these male head-butting rituals; and the year-end victors win the title of world champions. We have in human history often awarded women and their holdings to the victors of such wars.

If we can agree that we are a somewhat monogamous species, then we can assume that many human unions are long lasting. Long lasting relationships improve the chances for genetic transmissions, social membership, family or tribal safety, and food gathering, which then improve the species' chances for survival. Safety and food are primary, but without successful reproduction, they are meaningless. The continuation of human life then depends on the mating dance. And the mating dance is what is written in the stars. Female and male spinning eternally around each other, teasing, flirting, daring, mating: this is the same story that myths recount with great love and devotion.

In Robert Graves' book, *The White Goddess*, he discovers what for him becomes the basic monomyth for all mythologies. Although his work generally uses Celtic, Irish, and Welsh myths, his findings do ring true for other cultures. This monomyth concerns the goddess, the young king and the old king, to use Graves' description. This is a seasonal, vegetative myth which describes two men who vie for access to the woman-goddess through the early spring. It is necessary for the young king to overpower the old king and kill him. Then his blood and body parts are buried for the fertility of the land. The young king must depose the old king or the fertility of the fields will not take place. The old king goes to his death as gracefully as possible because there is divinity or immortality awaiting him upon his death. Burying him in or around the fields is symbolic of the procreative process on a mythic scale; the old king impregnates the goddess (as land) producing the new crops. The young king then reigns with the goddess throughout the coming year, only to be deposed and killed himself in the next spring by a new young king. This pattern of sacrifice represents a kind of sympathetic magic wherein a culture mimics the sex act between two people and the necessity of death for the creation of new life. Ancient peoples all around the world saw themselves in the earth's processes of creation, life, and death, all of which are necessary for survival into the next generation. These ancient impulses or instincts for survival are the strongest impulses humans have.

Back to the stars: in the night skies above, the eternal dance of male and female continues unabated. If humans did see themselves reflected in the stars, it was to see the best of both sexes. This egalitarian concept did not weigh the importance of one sex over the other. Instead, it established the necessity of both sexes as necessary to the survival of the human population. Each sex may have different responsibilities toward children or tribe, but each was seen as necessary. Even today, many scholars and psychologists and sociologists agree that both sexes must be utilized in the educating and the nurturing of the children. As Naomi Wolf writes in her book, *Fire With Fire*, the patriarchalists, those who believe in man's dominance, are being slowly replaced by an egalitarian revolution in which both sexes are considered necessary and equal in effectiveness. Nancy Chodorow writes in her book, *The Reproduction of Mothering*, that the only way to revolutionize parenting is to have both sexes contribute equally to the raising and the nurturing of children. Sara Ruddick in *Maternal Thinking* and Marilyn French in *The War Against Women* and *Beyond Power* write extensively that the solutions to world politics exist in giving women an equal voice. Patriarchal power is a human construct, not a divine one. It can be changed or modified like any other system of management. We do not see only Osiris in the sky; we must acknowledge the woman who turns the skies with him.

Ancient myths are the records of human experience and education. Passing on the lessons already learned increases the chances for human survival. Myths record cultural practices, acceptable and unacceptable behaviors, and most of all, the prioritization of the communal over the individual. All heroes, whether female or male, must return to the communal for verification of their experiences and their existence.

This sex revolution into an egalitarian construct of society will happen with or without the patriarchalists. This is a social revolution emerging from the lowest levels of society into the mainstream. And I believe that the primal instincts of human beings definitely come into play here. We cannot survive a one sexed society; there is no fertility in that, only sterility. Instinctually, we are moving toward the only social construct that can insure our survival: the egalitarian vision. But we cannot restore the family structure without addressing the community first. Humans are, and always have been, social creatures. We seek to belong to groups that define some purpose to our existence. This social instinct is so strong that even when the traditional social constructs fail, others arise to take their place. For example, the phenomenon of the absent father in current American society has greatly influenced the growth of gangs. These gangs provide structure, leadership, territory, and belonging: all the jobs that fathers are supposed to do for their children. In light of their absence, however, the natural instinct in these misguided children is to form their own societies to initiate themselves into some kind of social organization, especially if those organizations are threatening to the society of their fathers. In order to bring these people back into mainstream society, we must change our concepts about the modern isolation of the individual nuclear family, which has been a disaster. Humans did not form families first; instead, they formed social groups. It is the community and its components of ethical and moral behavior that strengthen the family. The nuclear family does not keep a society together. If there is no common community, the family cannot survive.

But the signs are promising for change. Disadvantaged neighborhoods, most made up of single parent families, are banding together to form a sense of community and security for their children. Some communities are beginning to police themselves. Some are concentrating their efforts to open more community centers for the young. Day care centers, neighborhood watch groups, even community or ethnic celebrations all serve to strengthen the sense of belonging. Now we also have computer dialogues along the internet and other electronic means, television talk shows, and televised news, all which serve to initiate and strengthen community dialogues. Communally, we are beginning to define the limitations society must impose upon its individual members so that the social body can survive and thrive. These dialogues, although we tend to think of them as pure cacaphonic noise, are the beginnings of these social discussions for the modern world. The more we talk, the more options we can discover that would allow us to solve our problems. Television itself has evolved into being the central tribal hearth fire that we sit around in the evening to get the news of the day, to hear the stories that teach us lessons, to share with each other the infinite commonalities of being human. The more we dialogue with each other, the greater our chances for survival.

It is the role of the hero to return to society with lessons learned from the personal quest. And though it is a personal quest, the lesson learned by all heroes is that ultimately, we are social animals who must sacrifice a portion of our individualities in order for our society to survive. A philosophy that only values individual wants and needs cannot contribute to the whole of the social fabric. Hero myths tell how we can make those sacrifices of ourselves in support of community wants and needs. The spiritual quest of the hero anchors the social quest, or if you will, the personal is the political. We need to recognize the hero myth for women and men -- not to support or establish a dominance of one over the other -- but to understand that women and men experience human life differently because of sex; the differences between man's kind of social action and women's kind of social action can only be understood from listening to each other's stories, the stories about our heroes.

The hero learns self awareness and social as well as personal responsibility. The hero becomes a moral, ethical being investing in the present with the experiences gained through the human condition. The hero also learns how to take responsibility for actions concerning self and community. The hero affirms that compensation must be paid for any living being that is taken or killed -- be that being animal, vegetable, or human. Lastly, the hero must develop compassion which should be the adhesive of any society. Without compassion, survival is impossible to achieve. Responsibility, compensation, and compassion are the mainstays for myths and the mainstays for human survival. And all myths, poetry, and literatures, whether the story of King Arthur and the Holy Grail or the Native American Buffalo Woman, teach those same values.

To argue the archetypal past is to understand the mythic connectors that affect us even today in our modern world. And although the fragmentation of cultural icons in the twentieth century has been duly recorded, I believe we are already beginning the creation of something new from their remains. Perhaps it will be a new structure, never before conceived. In any case, I know that the female heroes and the male heroes will be there to help direct us.

---

[1]Gimbutas, Marija. *The Language of the Goddess* (New York: Harper and Row, 1989) 265-266.

[2]Bronte, Charlotte. *Jane Eyre* (New York: Random House, 1944) 329.

Bibliography

Athanassakis, Aposolos N. *The Homeric Hymns*. Baltimore: Johns Hopkins
University Press, 1976.

Bachofen, J. J. *Myth, Religion, and Mother Right: Selected Writings of J.J.
Bachofen*. trans. by Ralph Manheim. Princeton: Princeton University Press,
1973.

Briffault, Robert. *The Mothers*. Abridged, with an introduction by Gordon Rattray
Taylor. New York: Atheneum, 1977.

Cameron, Averil and Amelie Kuhrt, eds. *Images of Women in Antiquity*. Detroit:
Wayne State University Press, 1983.

Campbell, Joseph. *The Hero With A Thousand Faces*. Princeton: Princeton
University Press, 1968.

————.*Historical Atlas of World Mythology*. New York: Harper & Row, 1988.

————.*The Masks of God: Occidental Mythology*. New York: Penguin Books,
1964.

————.*The Masks of God: Orientl Mythology*. New York: Penguin Books, 1964.

————.*The Masks of God: Primitive Mythology*. Princeton: Princeton University
Press, 1968.

Cixous, Helene and Catherine Clement. *The Newly Born Woman*. trans. by Betsy
Wing. Minneapolis: University of Minesota Press, 1975.

Chodorow, Nancy. *The Reproduction of Mothering: Psychoanalysis and the
Society of Gender*, Berkeley: University of California Press, 1979.

Daly, Mary. *Beyond God the Father: Toward a Philosophy of Women's
Liberation*. Boston: Beacon Press, 1977.

————.*Gyn-Ecology: The Metaethics of Radical Feminism*. Boston: Beacon
Press, 1978.

————.*Pure Lust: Elemental Feminist Philosophy*. Boston: Beacon Press, 1984.

Delaney, Janice, Mary Lupton, and Emily Toth. *The Curse: A Cultural History of
Menstruation*. Urbana: University of Illinois Press, 1988.

Dexter, Miriam Robbins. *Whence the Goddess: A Source Book*. New York:
Pergamon Press, 1990

Eisler, Riane. *The Chalice and the Blade: Our History, Our Future*. San
Francisco: Harper & Row, 1987.

Farrar, Janet and Stewart. *The Witches' Goddess*. Custer: Phoenix Publishing,
1987.

Frazer, Sir James George. *The Golden Bough: A Study of Magic and Religion*.
New York: Macmillan, 1963.

French, Marilyn. *Beyond Power: On Women, Men, and Morals*. New York:
Summit Books, 1985.

Gadon, Elinor W. *The Once and Future Goddess: A Symbol for Our Time*. San Francisco: Harper & Row. 1989.

Gimbutas, Marija. *The Goddesses and Gods of Old Europe: Myths and Cult Images*. Berkeley: University of California Press, 1982.

———.*The Language of the Goddess*. San Francisco: Harper & Row, 1989.

Goldenberg, Naomi. *Changing of the Gods*. Boston: Beacon Press, 1979.

Goodrich, Norma Lorre. *Priestesses*. New York: Harper Collins, 1989.

Graves, Robert. *The Greek Myths*. vol. 1&2. New York: Penguin Books, 1984.

———.*The White Goddess: A Historical Grammar of Poetic Myth*. New York: Farrar, Straus and Giroux, 1966.

Hadas, Moses, ed. *Greek Drama*. New York: Bantam, 1965.

Hall, Nor. *The Moon and the Virgin: Reflections on the Archetypal Feminine*. New York: Harper & Row, 1980.

Harding, M. Esther. *The Way of All Women*. Boston: Shambhala, 1990.

———.*Women's Mysteries: Ancient and Modern*. Boston: Shambhala, 1990.

Heilbrun, Carolyn. *Hamlet's Mother and Other Women*. New York: Columbia University Press, 1990.

Highwater, Jamake. *Myth and Sexuality*. Markham, Ontario: Penguin Books Canada Limited, 1990.

Johnson, Buffie. *Lady of the Beasts: Ancient Images of the Goddess and Her Sacred Animals*. San Francisco: Harper & Row, 1988.

Jung, Carl G. *The Archetypes and the Collective Unconscious*. trans.by R.F.C. Hull. Princeton: Princeton University Press, 1959.

———.*Man and His Symbols*. New York: Doubleday, 1964.

Keuls, Eva C. *The Reign of the Phallus: Sexual Politics in Ancient Athens*. New York: Harper & Row, 1979.

Kolbenshlag, Madonna. *Kiss Sleeping Beauty Good-Bye*. San Francisco: Harper & Row, 1979.

Kramer, Samuel Noah, ed. *Mythologies of the Ancient World*. New York: Doubleday,1961.

Lauter, Estella and Carol Schreier Rupprecht, eds. *Feminist Archetypal Theory: Interdisciplinary Re-Visons of Jungian Thought*. Knoxville: University of Tennessee Press, 1985.

Lerner, Gerda. *The Creation of Patriarchy*. New York: Oxford University Press, 1986.

Lichtman, Susan A. *Life Stages of Woman's Heroic Journey: A Study of the Origins of the Great Goddess Archetype*. Lewiston, New York: Edwin Mellen Press, 1991.

Monaghan, Patricia. *The Book of Goddesses and Heroines*. St. Paul: Llewellyn Press, 1990.

Neumann, Erich. *The Great Mother: An Analysis of the Archetype.* trans. by Ralph Mangeim. Princeton: Princeton University Press, 1963.

O'Barr, Jean F., Deborah Pope and Mary Wyer, eds. *Ties That Bind: Essays on Mothering and Patriarchy.* Chicago: University of Chicago Press, 1990.

Olson, Carl, ed. *The Book of the Goddess: Past and Present.* New York: Crossroads, 1989.

Perera, Syylvia Brinton. *Descent to the Goddess: A Way of Initiation for Women.* Toronto: InnerCity Books, 1981.

Plaskow, Judith and Carol P. Christ, eds. *Weaving the Visions: New Patterns in Feminist Spirituality.* San Francisco: Harper & Row, 1989.

Pomeroy, Sarah B. *Goddesses, Whores, Wives, and Slaves: Women in Classical Antiquity.* New York: Schocken Books, 1975.

Pratt, Annis P. *Archetypal Patterns in Women's Fiction.* Bloomington: Indiana University Press, 1981

Reed, Evelyn, "The Myth of Women's Inferiority" in *Problems of Women's Liberation.* New York: Merit, 1969..

Rich, Adrienne.*Of WomanBorn: Motherhood as Experience and Institution.* New York: W.W. Norton, 1977.

Ruddick, Sara. *Maternal Thinking: Toward a Politic of Peace.* New York: Ballentine Books, 1989.

Sjöö, Monica and Barbara Mor. *The Great Cosmic Mother: Rediscovering the Religion of the Earth.* San Francisco: Harper & Row, 1987.

Stone, Merlin. *When God Was A Woman.* New York: Harcourt, Brace & Jovanovich, 1976.

Trask, Haunani-Kay. *Eros and Power: The Promise of Feminist Theory.* Philadelphia: University of Pennsylvania Press, 1986.

Walker, Barbara G. *The Crone: Woman of Age, Wisdom, and Power.* San Francisco: Harper & Row, 1987.

———.*The Women's Dictionary of Symbols and Sacred Objects.* San Francisco: Harper & Row, 1988.

———.*The Women's Encyclopedia of Myths and Secrets.* New York: Harper & Row, 1983.

Washbourn, Penelope. *Becoming Woman: The Quest for Woleness in Female Experience.* New York: Harper & Row, 1977.

Wehr, Demaris S. *Jung & Feminism: Liberating Archetypes.* Boston: Beacon Press, 1987.

Wolkstein, Diana and Samuel Kramer. *Inanna: Queen of Heaven and Earth.* New York: Harper & Row, 1983.

WOMEN'S STUDIES